VEROEFFENTLICHUNGEN MITTELALTERLICHER MUSIKHANDSCHRIFTEN

NR. 4

PUBLICATIONS OF MEDIAEVAL MUSICAL MANUSCRIPTS

NO. 4

PARIS 13521 & 11411

Faksimile, Einleitung, Register und Transcriptionen aus den Handschriften PARIS, BIBL. NAT. NOUV. ACQ. FR. 13521 (La Clayette) und LAT. 11411

Von

Facsimile, Introduction, Index and Transcriptions from the manuscripts PARIS. BIBL. NAT. NOUV. ACQ. FR. 13521 (La Clayette) and LAT. 11411

By

LUTHER DITTMER

Institute of Mediaeval Music
1751 West 9th Street
Brooklyn 23, N. Y.
U. S. A.

An Edition of: 600 Copies

Eine Auflage von 600 Exemplaren

№ 500

Nouv. Acq. frç. 13521

Die um 1773 dem Marquis Nobelet de la Clayette gehörige, umfangreiche Sammelhandschrift war nicht aufzufinden, bis die Pariser Nationalbibliothek sie in 1952 erworben hat, wo sie heute die Signatur *nouv. acq. frç. 13521* trägt. Dieser Pergamentkodex (Grösse 26,5 x 18 cm.) weist 824 Seiten auf und besteht aus 36 Teilen. Von musikwissenschaftlichem Interesse sind die 30. und 31. Teile, die eine Ansammlung von Motetten aus dem späten dreizehnten Jahrhundert enthalten.

Die Motetten folgen einer Lücke in der Handschrift, nachdem der vorhergehende Teil auf S. 728b mitten in einer französischen Bearbeitung der Albigenserkriege von Pierre de Vaux-Cernay abbrach. Anscheinend ist die Motettensammlung vollständig, da die *recto* Seite (S. 729 = f. 369^r) mit einer Komposition am Anfang der ersten Spalte beginnt, während ein gleiches nur einmal wieder (S. 755 = f. 382^r) vorkommt. Die Sammlung selbst besteht aus lateinischen, französischen und gemischsprachigen Motetten, die in einer nicht vollkommenen Mensuralnotation aufgezeichnet sind, die der Notenschrift der älteren Motettenfaszikel der Montpellier Handschrift gleicht 1). Abweichend von den meisten Motettenhandschriften, findet sich die Aufzeichnung der Kompositionen in Kollumnen, wobei es öfters vorkommt, dass eine Motette bis zur folgenden *verso* Seite reicht, was zeigt, dass dieser Kodex nicht für den praktischen Gebrauch angefertigt war.

Auch inhaltlich ist der Clayette Kodex mit dem alten Korpus der Montpellier Handschrift verwandt, da beide Werke neueren Stils (mit belebten *tripla,* die kleinere Notenwerte anwenden) ausschliessen, und vorwiegend die, in den Notre-Dame Choralbearbeitungen vorkommenden Choralausschnitte für Tenores benützen, wenn die Motetten selbst nicht direkt auf Klauseln gehen.

1) Vgl. meinen Aufsatz: ***The Ligatures of the Montpellier Manuscript,*** in ***Musica Disciplina,*** IX 1955.

Nouv. Acq. Frç. 13521

The comprehensive composite manuscript, which belonged to the Marquis de la Clayette about the year 1773 could not be located until the National Library in Paris purchased it in 1952; this codex today is known by the call-number *nouv. acq. frç. 13521.* This vellum manuscript (dimensions 26.5 x 18 cm.) contains 824 pages and is divided into 36 sections. The 30th and 31st divisions are of musicological interest, and contain a collection of motets from the late thirteenth century.

The motets follow a lacuna in the manuscript, after the previous section broke off on p. 728b in the middle of a French adaptation of the Albigensian wars by Pierre de Vaux-Cernay. Apparently , the motet collection is complete, since the first recto (p. 729 = f. 369^r) begins with a composition at the head of the first column, whereas this occurs only once again in the course of these sections: (p. 755 = f. 382^r). The collection itself consists of Latin, French and polyglot motets, which are written in a partially mensural notation, which resembles that of the older fascicles of the Montpellier manuscript 1). The manner of arranging the compositions on the page is at variance with that of most of the motet codices, since the compositions are presented in collumns, whereby it quite often occurs that a motet extends to the following *verso*; this indicates that this codex was not prepared for practical usage.

The Clayette manuscript, however, is also related internally to the old corpus of the Montpellier manuscript, since both sources exclude compositions of the newer style (with lively *tripla,* which utilise smaller note values), while using for the main part only those passages from plain chant as tenores, which are to be found in the Notre-Dame *organa,* whereby the en-

1) Confice my article: ***The Ligatures of the Montpellier Manuscript,*** in ***Musica Disciplina,*** IX 1955.

Doch kommen die Kompositionen des sechsten Faszikels der Montpellier Handschrift, der nur zweistimmige Motetten enthält, mit dem Repertoire dieses Kodex nicht in Berührung. Wie in den anderen bekannten, mensural aufgezeichnetenHand - schriften des ausgehenden 13. Jahrhunderts, wird die dreistimmige, Form der Motette mit verschiedenen Texten in den Oberstimmen vorgezogen, wenn auch vierstimmige Kompositionen mit drei Texten in den Oberstimmen vertreten sind.

Auch wenn die Neuentdeckung dieser Handschrift eine grössere Fülle von Material zur Erforschung der Musik dieser Epoche bringt, mehr als alle anderen Funde unseres Jahrzehnts, so vermehren die enthaltenen Kompositionen das uns sonst überlieferte Repertoire der Zeit nur um eine vollständige Komposition *Cil qui m'aime/Quant chantent oisiaus/Portare* Nr. 43, und einige Kontrafacta, sowie neue Stimmen. Die meisten Kompositionen sind in den Faszikeln 2-5 der Montpellier Handschrift bekannt, wo sie konsequenter (und öfters richtiger) aufgeschrieben sind; sonst sind einige in den früheren, die französische Motette enthaltenden Kodices bekannt: *Wolfenbüttel 1099,* sowie Paris, *Bibliothèque nationale frç. 844* und *12615*. Für Kompositionen, die sonst nur in der letzten Gruppe vertreten sind, bieten diese Versionen den Vorteil, dass sie nur hier mensural notiert sind, was die Transcription wesentlich erleichtert. Die Clayette Handschrift überliefert deswegen, die Kompositionen des Hauptstromes des mehrstimmigen Schaffens Frankreichs der Mitte des 13. Jahrhunderts und ist konservativ genug die Motetten mit der verzierten, in kleinen Notenwerten verlaufenden *tripla* zu vermeiden.

In der Literatur konnte diese Quelle bisher nach einer Textkopie zitiert werden, die für den Pariser Forscher La Curne de Sainte Palaye angefertigt wurde, und die in Pariser Bibliotheken aufbewahrt ist. Die französischen Texte der Motetten sind mit kleinen Fehlern in der Papierhandschrift der Arsenalbibliothek *6361* kopiert. Abschriften der anderen Teile der Handschrift sind in der Nationalbibliothek *Coll. Moreau 1715-1719* zu finden. Dank des ausführlichen

tire motet may also be derived from a clausula. The compositions of the sixth fascicle of the Montpellier manuscript, which contains settings for only two voices, however, are not represented in the repertoire of this codex. As in the case of the other mensural manuscripts which are known from the end of the 13th century, the three-voiced form of the motet with different texts in the upper-voices is preferred, although compositions for four parts with three texts in the upper voices are also represented.

Even though the rediscovery of this manuscript offers us a larger fund of material for research into the music of this epoch, more than all of the other discoveries of this decade, the compositions contained in this source add only one completely new composition to the repertoire of the time: *Cil qui m'aime/ Quant chantent oisiaus/Portare* No. 43, in addition to some contrafacta and new voices. Most of the compositions are also found in fascicles 2-5 of the Montpellier manuscript, where they are notated more consequently (and often more correctly); otherwise, some compositions are found in those earlier codices, which contain French motets: *Wolfenbüttel 1099* and Paris, *Bibliothèque nationale frç. 844* and *12615*. As far as those compositions are concerned, which are otherwise only to be found in this last group of sources, the versions of these motets in the Clayette codex have the advantage, that they are available in a mensural setting only in this source, which naturally greatly simplifies their transcription. Thus, the Clayette manuscript presents an anthology of the compositions of the main stream of polyphonic creativity in France of the middle of the 13th century, and is still conservative enough to avoid motets with *tripla* that are highly ornamented and utilise smaller note values.

This source has been quoted in the scientific literature until now according to a copy of the texts, which had been made for the Parisian researcher La Curne de Sainte Palaye and which is preserved in Parisian libraries. The French texts (with smaller inaccuracies) have been copied into the paper manuscript, *Bibliothèque de l'Arsenal 6361*. Copies of the other parts of the

Inhaltsverzeichnisses der letzt genannten Sammlung ist es Friedrich Ludwig [1] gelungen, die Handschrift grösstenteils mit ungemeiner Präzision zu rekonstruieren. Teilweise gehen diese Notizen auf seine Ausführungen zurück. An Hand der Abschrift der Motettentexte, hat G. Raynaud die französischen Texte in seinem *Recueil* [2] veröffentlicht. Über den Aufbau der Handschrift, vergleiche man Paul Meyer, *Notices* [3]. Die, die Motetten betreffenden Notizen wurden auch von Y. Rokseth in ihrer Ausgabe der Montpellier Handschrift [4] abgedruckt.

An neuerer Literatur (d.h. nachdem die Handschrift von der Pariser Nationalbibliothek erworben war) findet man ein Verzeichnis des Inhaltes neben anderen Notizen von A. Rosenthal [5], und eine Besprechung der Komposition *Alma iugi/His hec ratio/Caro spiritui* von L. Schrade [6]. Zu dem Problem der Entdeckung der sonst unbekannten Tenores, vgl. *Die Musikforschung,* IX 1956 Heft IV. Der zu früh verstorbene Forscher, M. Bukofzer, hatte einen umfassenden Aufsatz über diese Handschrift in Aussicht gestellt. Es ist ihm noch gelungen einen Anfang davon gemacht zu haben, der nach seinem Tod in den *Annales musicologiques* (IV 1957 S. 255ff.) veröffentlicht worden ist.

Im folgenden gebe ich nur ein alphabetisch geordnetes Verzeichnis der Textanfänge der einzelnen Stimmen der verschiedenen Kompositionen an, las die Seitenzahl,

1) *Repertorium organorum recentioris et motetorum vetustissimi stili,* Band I, Teil 2 (unveröffentlicht) S. 408-421; eine neue vervollständigte Ausgabe dieses Werkes wurde vom Verfasser vorgenommen.

2) *Recueil de motets français,* 1883, Band II, S. 39-47.

3) Notice sur deux anciens mss. francais ayant appartenu au marquis de la Clayette in *Notices et extraits des mss. de la Bibl. nat.,* erster Teil 1890 S. 1-10.

4) Y. Rokseth, *Polyphonies du 13e siècle,* I-IV, 1936-1939.

5) *Annales musicologiques,* I 1953, S. 105ff.

6) *Speculum,* XXX 1955, S. 393ff.

codex are preserved in the *Bibliothèque nationale, Coll. Moreau 1715-1719.* Because of the detailed table of contents of the latter collection, Friedrich Ludwig [1] was able to reconstruct this manuscript for the most part with unusual precision. These notes are based partially on his comments. From the copy of the texts, G. Raynaud was ablt to publish the French texts in his *Recueil* [2]. Concerning the construction of the codex, confice Paul Meyer *Notices* [3]. Information concerning the motets was reprinted by Y. Rokseth in her edition of the Montpellier manuscript [4].

As far as newer literature is concerned (*id est,* that written since the manuscript was purchased by the National Library in Paris), one finds an index of the contents along with other information by A. Rosenthal [5], and a discussion of the composition *Alma iugi/His hec ratio/Caro spiritui* by L. Schrade [6]. Concerning the problem of the identification of the tenores which are otherwise unknown confice *Die Musikforschung,* IX 1956 Heft IV. The great researcher, M. Bukofzer, who died out of time, envisiaged a comprehensive essay on this manuscript. He succeeded in beginning such a work, which was published posthumously in the *Annales musicologiques* (IV 1956, p. 255ff.).

Below, I have given a list arranged alphabetically of the textual incipits of the individual voices of the various compositions contained in this manuscript, whereby

1) *Repertorium organorum recentioris et motetorum vetustissimi stili,* Vol. I, part 2 (unpublished) pp. 408-421; a new completed edition of this work has been undertaken by the author.

2) *Recueil de motets français,* 1883, Vol. II pp. 39-47.

3) Notice sur deux anciens mss. francais ayant appartenu au marquis de la Clayette in *Notices et extraits des mss. de la Bibl. nat.,* part I 1890, pp. 1-10

4) Y. Rokseth, *Polyphonies du 13e siecle,* Vol. I-IV, 1936-1939.

5) *Annales musicologiques,* I 1953, p. 105ff.

6) *Speculum,* XXX 1955, p. 393ff.

Nummer des Oberstimmentextes oder Klassifikation des Tenors (stets nach Ludwig 1)), sowie die Zugänglichkeit der Übertragungen vermittelt. Sollte eine Komposition meines Wissens noch nicht in Übertragung geboten werden, so sind die Nebenquellen angegeben. Zwei Kompositionen werden in Übertragung angeführt.

Latin 11411

Diese Fragmentensammlung bietet uns in ff. 44-45 (neufoliert) ein Doppelblatt, möglicherweise, aber nicht unbedingt, die Mitte einer Lage, wovon sonstige Reste nicht aufzufinden sind. Die Aufzeichnungsart ist vollkommen mensural, und die Kompositionen sind in Partitur notiert. Die einzige Erwähnung dieser kleinen Sammlung in der Fachliteratur fand ich in Y. Rokseth, *Polyphonies du 13e siècle*, IV 1939, S. 56-57, sowie unter Komposition Nr. 60. Sie stammt aus dem frühen 14. Jahrhundert.

Der Inhalt schliesst ein:

1. f. 44^r Ein *Sanctus* zu zwei.
2. f. 44^v Ein *Agnus dei* zu drei.
3. f. 45^r Ein Hoquetus *Sustine* zu drei.
4. f. 45^v Der Tropus *Crimina tollis* zum *Agnus dei* zu drei.
5. f. 45^v Der Anfang des Oberbaues der Motette *Psallat Chorus* zu drei.

1) Die Tenores werden nach ihrer Herkunft aufgezählt, wobei M sich auf Notenfolgen aus Messkompositionen, O aus Offiziumsgesängen bezieht, und die steigende Nummerierung der Anordnung der Choralbearbeitungen in der Handschrift Florenz, *Biblioteca Mediceo-Laurenziana, pluteo 29,1* angepasst ist. Die steigenden Motettennummern berücksichtigen die Anordnung der Tenores (zuerst Messkompositionen) und versucht innerhalb einer jeden Gruppe die Entstehungszeit eines jeden Motettenkomplexes darzustellen. Da die Handschrift eine parallele Folierung und Paginierung aufweist, werden beide angegeben. Schrade, *a.a.O.*, wies darauf hin, dass die von Rosenthal als drei verschiedene Kompositionen aufgeführten Texte Nr. III-V eigentlich nur eine Motette (?) bilden; um nicht die folgende Aufzählung von Rosenthal zu ändern und mehr Verwirrung in die Benennung der Kompositionen zu bringen, haben wir ihre sonstige Benennung beibehalten, soweit richtig. Folgende Abkürzungen werden angewandt: Mot = Motetus; Qua = Quadruplum; T = Tenor; Tr = Triplum.

reference is made to the page in the codex, the number of the text of upper-voices or the classification of the tenor (always according to Ludwig 1)), as well as to the availability of transcriptions. If a composition is not known to me in a published transcription, a list of the subsidiary sources is given. Two compositions are transcribed here.

Latin 11411

This collection of fragments contains in ff. 44-45 (new foliation) a bifolio, probably but not necessarily the middle of a gathering; further remnants of this source have not been discovered. The notation is completely mensural, and the compositions are presented in score. The only mention of these fragments in the scientific literature, that I have discovered, is contained in Y. Rokseth, *Polyphonies du 13e siècle*, IV 1939, pp. 56-57 and under composition No. 60. These leaves spring from the 14th century.

The contents include:

1. f. 44^r A *Sanctus* a 2.
2. f. 44^v An *Agnus dei* a 3.
3. f. 45^r An hoquetus *Sustine* a 3.
4. f. 45^v The trope *Crimina tollis* to the *Agnus* a 3.
5. f. 45^v The beginning of the upper-voices of the motet *Psallat chorus* a 3.

1) The tenores are listed according to their source of origin, whereby M indicates successions of notes taken from settings of the mass, and O from compositions in the offices; the enumeration represents the succession of *organa* in the manuscript Florence, *Biblioteca Mediceo-Laurenziana, pluteo 29,1*. Ascending motet numbers reflect the arrangement of tenores (beginning with settings from the mass) and attempts within each group to present the chronological succession of each complex of motets. Since this codex has both a foliation and a pagination, both will be given. Schrade, *loco citato*, drew attention to the fact that what Rosenthal had held to be three different compositions, texts III-V, actually form one motet (?); so that we do not disturb the further enumeration of Rosenthal and bring more confusion into the designation of the compositions, we have retained Rosenthal's order, in so far as it is correct. The following abbreviations are used: Mot = Motetus; Qua = Quadruplum; T = Tenor; Tr = Triplum.

Die ersten drei Kompositionen sind mir in anderen Quellen unbekannt, dafür konnte keine liturgische Melodie in den ersten zwei Kompositionen von mir festgestellt werden. Der Choralausschnitt des Tenors des Hoquetus Nr. 3 entstammt dem *Alleluia V Dulce lignum* (M 22), wo er öfters auch *portare* heisst, (*sustine* ist richtiger als *sustinere* als Bezeichnung dieser Komposition, da die Tenornotenfolge sich nicht auf die mit der Silbe *re* versehenen Note erstreckt). Nr. 4 ist uns in verschiedenen Fassungen in spanischen und schweizer Quellen bekannt, wo sie öfters mit dem *Agnus dei* Nr. XII verbunden wird. Zur Literatur und sonstigen Übertragungen vgl. H. Anglès, *El Códex musical de Las Huelgas,* 1931 unter Nr. 23. Zur Literatur von Nr. 5, vgl. Y. Rokseth, *a.a.O.* unter Nr. 60.

Ich halte diese anfangs des 14. Jahrhunderts geschriebenen Fragmente für englische Provenienz, da (1) mehrstimmige Bearbeitungen des *ordinarium missae* um diese Zeit in den grossen Zentren Frankreichs unbekannt sind, während sie in peripheren Kreisen, besonders auf den britischen Inseln blühten. (2) Die Verzierungsart der textlosen Partien ist uns in einer Reihe von Handschriftenresten in England bekannt (besonders unter den Worcester Fragmenten [1]). (3) Die kurzen, formelhaften, oft wiederholten Sequenzen, die auf- oder abwärts immer auf die nächste Tonstufe steigen, scheinen mehr in England angewandt worden zu sein als auf dem Kontinent (vgl. dazu Worcester Nr. 31). (4) Die Motette Nr. 5 ist auch in englischen Quellen bekannt [2] und kann auch dort entstanden sein. (5) Der ausgesprochene binäre Rhythmus der dritten Komposition ist noch zu dieser Zeit ein Hinweis für den insularen Ursprung.

1) Vgl. L. A. Dittmer, *The Worcester Fragments,* 1957. Weitere Facsimiles dieser Kompositionen sind in Band V dieser Reihe veröffentlicht.

2) *Westminster Abbey 33327* Nr. 8, facsimiliert in Band V dieser Reihe.

The first three compositions are unknown to me in other sources, and I was unable to identify any liturgical sequence of notes in the first two compositions. The plain chant excerpt used as the tenor for No. 3 is taken from the *Alleluia V Dulce lignum* (M 22) where it is otherwise often called *portare,* (*sustine* is more acurate as a designation for this composition than *sustinere,* since the succession of tenor notes used does not include the tones sung to the syllable *re*). No. 4 is also found in different versions in Spanish and Swiss sources, where this composition is often connected with *Agnus dei* No. XII. Concerning the literature affecting this composition and further transcriptions, confice H. Anglès, *El Códex musical de Las Huelgas,* 1931 under No. 23. For the literature concerned with No. 5, confice Y. Rokseth, *opere citato* under No. 60.

I consider these fragments, written at the beginning of the 14th century to be of English provenience, since (1) polyphonic settings of the *ordinarium missae* are unknown at this time in the larger centers in France, whereas they flourished in peripheral circles, especially in the British Isles; (2) the type of ornamentation used for the textless passages is known to us in a series of fragments in England (especially among the Worcester Fragments [1]); (3) the short, formula-like, often repeated sequences, which move upwards and downwards onto neighboring pitches appear to have been used more in England than on the continent (confice Worcester No. 31); (4) the motet No. 5 is also known in English sources [2] and can have originated there; (5) the definite binary rhythm of the third composition is still at this time an indication for insular origin; (6) the presence of a composition also known in Spanish and Swiss sources

1) Confice L. A. Dittmer, *The Worcester Fragments,* 1957. Further facsimiles of these compositions are printed in Vol. V of this series.

2) *Westminster Abbey 33327* No. 8.; facsimile in Vol. V of this series.

(6) Das Vorkommen einer Komposition, die auch in spanischen und schweizer Quellen bekannt ist, schliesst nicht aus, dass diese Kompositionen ebenso in England vertreten waren, da die Repertoires dieser Länder viele Berührungspunkte miteinander aufweisen. Übrigens, das Fehlen der englischen Notationsweise (Rauten statt Puncta, englische Nebenform der Coniunctura, usw.) besagt nichts, da die kontinentalen Notationsformen schon lange in England verwendet wurden.

Im folgenden biete ich Transcriptionen der ersten vier Kompositionen an. Besonders möchte ich den Hoquetus Nr. 3 hervorheben, der auch von Rokseth, *a.a.O.* IV, S. 56 besprochen wurde. Ein ähnlicher Hoquetus befindet sich in der Handschrift Montpellier *H 196* (Nr. 5), wo er *portare* bezeichnet wird. Die zwei Hoqueti haben nur den Tenor und teilweise die Tenorformel gemeinsam. Sonst ist kein zwingender Grund vorhanden, anzunehmen, dass der Komponist der einen Weise von dem anderen Hoquetus beeinflusst wurde. Nach Aufzeichnung der Pausen ist der vorliegende Hoquetus als in einem binären Modus aufzufassen. Dieser Modus wird auch durch die Anwendung von Puncta für beide die *longa* teilende *breves* bezeugt, auch in Fällen wo *punctum virga* in einem ternären Modus vorgezogen wären. Der Tenor wird vier Mal vorgetragen, wobei die geraden Durchführungen eine andere Gruppierung innerhalb der Formel aufweisen als die ungeraden. Im Sinne des 13. Jahrhunderts bedeutet das nichts besonders, und dementsprechend soll man nicht von *color* und *talea* reden, als wenn diese Komposition schon der *ars nova* angehörte.

Verzeichnis der Motetten in 13521

Übertragungen der meisten Kompositionen befinden sich in Y. Rokseth, *Polyphonies du 13e siècle*, II-III 1936. Einige weitere in P. Aubry, *Cent Motets du 13e siècle*, 1908. Vereinzelte in L. Schrade, *Speculum*, XXX 1955 S. 411 und Inzipien auch in L. Dittmer, *Robert de Handlo*, 1959. * bezeichnet Kompositionen deren Tenorquelle nicht unter den Notre-Dame Choral-

does not exclude the fact, that this composition was also represented in England, since the répertoire of these countries exhibit many points of contact. Finally, the absence of the English notational dialect (rhomboids instead of squares, English form of the *coniunctura* etc.) is not significant since the continental notational forms had been used in England for quite some time.

I have offered below transcriptions of the first four compositions. I should like to draw attention to the hoquetus No. 3, which Rokseth, *opere citato,* IV p. 56 has also discussed. A similar hoquetus can also be found in the manuscript Montpellier *H 196* (No. 5), where it is designated as *portare*. The two hoqueti only have the tenor succession and partially the tenor formula in common. Otherwise there is no compelling reason to assume that the composer of the one setting was influenced by the other composition. According to the arrangement of the rests, the present hoquetus is written in a binary mode. This is shown by the use of *puncta* for both of the *breves* which divide the *longa,* even in such cases where *punctum virga* would have been preferred in a ternary mode. The tenor is presented four times, whereby the even numbered statements have a different grouping of notes within the rhythmic formula than the odd ones. This is not especially significant in the sense of the 13th century, and consequently one should not speak of *color* and *talea,* as if this composition already belonged to the *ars nova.*

Index of the Motets in 13521

Transcriptions of most of the compositions are to be found in 6. Rokseth, *Polyphonies du 13e siècle,* II-III 1936. Additional ones also in P. Aubry, *Cent Motets du 13e siècle,* 1908. Others in L. Schrade, *Speculum,* XXX 1955 p. 411 and incipits also in L. Dittmer, *Robert de Handlo,* 1959. * designates compositions, the sources of whose tenores are not to be found among

bearbeitungen zu finden sind; § eine sonst unbekannte Stimme einer weiteren uns bekannten Komposition; † ein Tenor, der in dieser Komposition sonst nicht bekannt ist; ‡ eine Zusatznummer zu Ludwigs *Repertorium*; d und t = duplum und triplum (wenn der Text anderwärtig für beide Stimmen benutzt wird); con = conductus. Handschriften: *N* = Paris, *Bibl. nat. frç. 12615*; *R* = *ibidem 844*; *W2* = Wolfenbüttel, *Helmstedt 1099*.

the Notre-Dame *organa*; § an otherwise unknown voice of a composition known elsewhere; † a tenor, which is otherwise unknown in this setting; ‡ a number added to Ludwig's *Repertorium*; d and t = duplum and triplum (when the text is used elsewhere for both voices); con = conductus. Manuscripts: *N* = Paris, *Bibl. nat. frç. 12615*; *R* = *ibidem 844*; *W2* = Wolfenbüttel, *Helmstedt 1099*.

Text Anfang Textual Incipit	Nr. No.	Stimme Voice	Ludwig Nr. Ludwig No.	Übertragung Transcription
A ce que dist bien	40	Tr	520	Rokseth 93
Agmina	24	T	M 65*	Dittmer
Agmina milicie	24	Mot	532	Dittmer
Alleluia	14	T	M 79*	Rokseth 58
Alleluia (= Domino)	19	T	unid.	Rokseth 40
Amours mi font rejoir	33	Tr	‡(99a)	Dittmer
Amours mi font soffrir	47	Tr	664	Rokseth 111
Amoris	50	T	M 27	Rokseth 86
Angelus	56	T	M 20	Rokseth 39
Anima iugi lacrimas	3	Con	--	Schrade
Au coumencement d'este	14	Mot	118	Rokseth 88
Aucuns m'ont par leur	56	Mot	263	Aubry 36
Au douz mois de mai	20	Tr	275	Rokseth 41
Ave beatissima civitas	38	Tr	394	Rokseth 55
Ave deitatis templum	12	Qua	‡(511a)	§ *Cele m'a tolu*
Ave gloriosa mater	1	Mot	804	Rokseth 53
Ave lux luminum ave	21	Tr	784	Rokseth 56
Ave Maria gratia plena	38	Mot	395	Rokseth 55
Ave maris stella (= Iohanne)	38	T	M 29	Rokseth 55
Ave virgo regia mater	1	Tr	805	Rokseth 53
Bele sanz orgueil	40	Mot	519	Rokseth 93
Benedicta	7	T	M 32	*W2* f. 221v
Biau cuers saverus	10	Mot	800	Rokseth 30
Caro spiritui quid	3	Con	--	Schrade
Ce fu en tres douz tens	27	Tr	‡,(451a)	*F* f. 398r: *In veritate*
Cele m'a tolu la vie	11	Tr	511	Rokseth 78
C'est quadruble sanz	10	Qua	798	Rokseth 30
Chant d'oiseaus et fuel	49	Mot	177	Rokseth 87
Chascuns dist que je	39	Tr	149	*W2* f. 215r, *N* f. 183v
Cil qui m'aime et si	43	Tr	‡(306a)	Unicum
Crux forma penitentie	20	Mot	274	Rokseth 41
Cumque	37	T	O 31	Rokseth 92
Dame de valour regart	32	Tr	71	Rokseth 90
Dame vostre douz regart	32	Mot	72	Rokseth 90
De la virge Katerine	24	Qua	536	Dittmer
Demenant grant joie	6	Mot	84	Rokseth 74
Deus fidem seminat	41	Mot	495	Aubry 62
Diex de chante maintenant	49	Tr	176	Rokseth 87
Diex je n'en partire	54	Mot	828	Rokseth 79
Domino	1	T	B.D.1	Rokseth 53
Doucete sui brune et	45	Mot	685	Rokseth 129
Douz rossignolet joliz	22	Tr	541	Rokseth 38
Eius	45	T	O 16	Rokseth 129
Eius	53	T	O 16	Rokseth 22
El mois d'avril qu'ivers	30	Qua	318	Rokseth 36
Encontre le tens de	41	Tr	496	Rokseth 95
En doit fine amour	48	Tr	187	Rokseth 134
En mai q.r.e.f. par matin	34	Mot	236	Rokseth 121
En mai q.r.e.f. que joi	47	Mot	663	Rokseth 111

Et exaltavi	40	T	M 51	Rokseth 93
Et gaudebit	30	T	M 24	Rokseth 36
Et super	11	T	M 66*	Rokseth 78
Et super	16	T	M 66*	Rokseth 110
Fiat	10	T	‡O 51*	Rokseth 30
Florebit	35	T	†M 53	Trans. S. 12
Flos filius eius	8	T	O 16	Rokseth 109
Flos filius eius	9	T	O 16	Rokseth 127
Flos filius eius	25	T	O 16	Rokseth 21
Flos filius eius	47	T	O 16	Rokseth 111
Gentes	52	T	†‡M 96*	Trans. S. 63
He desloials mesdisant	55	Mot	279	Rokseth 81
Hec dies	15	T	M 13	Rokseth 88
Hec (dies)	51	T	M 13	Rokseth 45
He Dieu de si haut si bas	37	Tr	708	Rokseth 92
He Diex tant sui de joie	52	Mot	‡(632b)	Trans. S. 63
He quant je remir son cors	50	Mot	361	Rokseth 86
In Bethleem	33	T	M 8	Dittmer
In Bethleem Herodes	33	Mot	98	Dittmer
In odorem	41	T	M 45	Rokseth 95
In omni fratre tuo non	23	Mot	197	Rokseth 37
In salvatoris nomine qui	27	Qua	452	Rokseth 57
In seculum	23	T	M 13	Rokseth 37
In seculum	39	T	M 13	*W2* f. 215v, *N* f. 183v
In seculum	42	T	M 13	Rokseth 28
In seculum	44	T	M 13	Rokseth 138
In seculum	46	T	M 13	Rokseth 137
In seculum	48	T	M 13	Rokseth 134
In seculum	49	T	M 13	Rokseth 87
In veritate	2	T	M 37	Rokseth 52
In veritate comperi quod	27	Mot	451	Rokseth 57
Iustus	29	T	M 53	Rokseth 32
Ja de bonne amour mes cuers	18	Mot	282	Rokseth 91
Ja n'amerai autre que	46	Tr	211	Rokseth 137
Ja pour mal que puisse	55	Tr	278	Rokseth 81
Je ai les maus d'amours	44	Tr	188	Rokseth 138
Je ne puis plus durer	29	Mot	523	Rokseth 32
Joie et soulaz ne me vaut	45	Tr	684	Rokseth 129
La beaute ma dame le cuer	48	Mot	186	Rokseth 134
L'atrier m'esbatoie	6	Tr	83	Rokseth 74
Latus	34	T	M 14	Rokseth 121
L'autrier j.m.a. en un v.	57	Mot	780	Rokseth 112
L'autrier j.m.a. par un dest	25	Mot	651	Rokseth 21
Le bergier si grant envie	53	Mot	657	Rokseth 22
Le premier jor de mai	29	Qua	521	Rokseth 32
Letabitur	22	T	M 66*	Rokseth 38
Li dous maus m'ocit que	42	Qua	146	Rokseth 28
Lis hec ratio tuo iudicio	3	Con	--	Schrade
Lonc tens a que ne vi	11	Mot	512	Rokseth 78
Lonc tens ai mise	15	Tr	117	Rokseth 88
Ma loialtez m'a nusi	42	Mot	147	Rokseth 28
Manere	6	T	M 5	Rokseth 74
Manere	32	T	M 5	Rokseth 90
Maubatu longuement pleure	37	Mot	707	Rokseth 92
Mellis stilla maris stella	19	Mot	808	Rokseth 40
Mens fidem (= Deus fidem)				
Moine qui a cuer jolif	16	Mot	550	Rokseth 110
Molt m'abelist l'amorous	8	Mot	674	Rokseth 109
Mors	13	T	M 18	Rokseth 35
Mors a primi patris vitio	13	Qua	256	Rokseth 35
Mors morsu nata	13	Mot	255	Rokseth 35
Mors que stimulo nos	13	Tr	254	Rokseth 35
Mout ai este en doulour	36	Mot	378	Rokseth 130
Mout loiaument l'ai	7	Tr	407	§Cf: *Se longuement*
Mout m'a fait cruieus	52	Tr	‡(632a)	Trans. S. 63

Mout me fait grief le d.	23	Tr	196	Rokseth 37
Mout souvent m'ont	36	Tr	377	Rokseth 130
Mulier omnis peccati	28	Mot	30	Rokseth 24 Text: *E non*
Mulierum	36	T	M 29	Rokseth 130
Neuma	21	T	unid.	Rokseth 21
Neuma	54	T	unid.	Rokseth 79
Nonne sanz amor n'avra	16	Tr	549	Rokseth 110
Nostrum	26	T	M 44	Rokseth 19
O Maria, maris stella	2	Mot	448	Rokseth 52
O Maria, mater pia vite	30	Tr	‡(317a)	§Cf. *El mois*
O Maria, virgo davitica	2	Tr	449	Rokseth 52
O quam sancta, quam benigna	30	Mot	317	Rokseth 36
Omnes	28	T	M 1	Rokseth 24
Onqes n'ama loialment	8	Tr	675	Rokseth 109
Par matin s'est levee	35	Tr	‡(528a)	Trans. S. 12
Par un matin me levai	28	Tr	522	Rokseth 32
Par un matinet l'autrier	53	Qua	658	Rokseth 22
Par une matinee el mois	19	Tr	807	Rokseth 40
Perlustravit	31	T	unid.	Rokseth 27
Plus bele que flors est	25	Qua	652	Rokseth 21
Portare	43	T	†M 22	Unicum
Portare	55	T	M 22	Rokseth 81
Pro patribus	17	T	M 30	Rokseth 89
Pour renvoisier et pour moi	28	Tr	28	Rokseth 24
Pour vos amie crieng	50	Tr	362	Rokseth 86
Povre secours ai encore	56	Tr	265	Rokseth 39
Quant chantent oisiaus	43	Mot	‡(306b)	Unicum
Quant define la verdour	9	Tr	661	Rokseth 127
Quant froidure trait a fin	24	Tr	535	Dittmer
Quant naist la flor en	11	Tr	637	Rokseth 31
Quant repaire la douçour	9	Mot	662	Rokseth 127
Quant revient et foille	25	Tr	650	Rokseth 21
Quant voi le douz tens	34	Tr	235	Rokseth 121
Quant vois remirant	51	Tr	126	Rokseth 45
Que ferai biau sire Diex	44	Mot	189	Rokseth 138
Qui d'amours veut bien	26	Tr	218	Rokseth 19
Qui la voudroit lonc tens	26	Qua	220	Rokseth 19
Qui longuement pourroit	26	Mot	219	Rokseth 19
Qui voudroit fame esprover	11	Qua	639	Rokseth 31
Res nova mirabilis virgo	14	Tr	582	Rokseth 58
Salve virgo rubens rosa	21	Mot	783	Rokseth 56
Seculorum amen	57	T	‡(O 52)	Rokseth 112
Se j'ai ame folement	39	Mot	150	*W2* f. 215^v
Se j'ai servi longuement	17	Tr	396	Rokseth 89
Se longuement ai de m'amie	7	Mot	406	*W2* f. 221^v
Sire Diex li doux maus	46	Mot	212	Rokseth 137
Sire qui vos vantez	53	Tr	659	Rokseth 22
Sustinere	18	T	M 22	Rokseth 91
Sustinere	20	T	M 22	Rokseth 41
Tanquam	11	T	O 2	Rokseth 31
Tanquam suscipit vellud	11	Mot	636	Rokseth 31 Text: *Deboinerement*
Tres douce pensee qui	35	Mot	‡(528b)	Trans. S. 12
Trois s.s.r.m...l'ainne	31	Mot	919	Rokseth 27
Trois s.s.r.m...la jonete	31	Qua	921	Rokseth 27
Trois s.s.r.m...la mainnee	31	Tr	920	Rokseth 27
Trop ai lonc tens en folie	42	Tr	148	Rokseth 28
Trop longuement m'a failli	17	Mot	397	Rokseth 58
Veritatem	27	T	M 37	Rokseth 57
Virgo decus castitatis	14	Mot	583	Rokseth 89
Virgo gloriosa, forma	22	Mot	542	Rokseth 38
Virgo virginum, lumen	51	Mot	127	Rokseth 45
Vos ni dormirez james	10	Tr	799	Rokseth 30

n. a. frç. 13521 Nr. 35

Par matin s'est levee Tres douce pensee Florebit

25
ee. 'Mes a - mis mi - gnoz Qui ma en - si ba -
Mes Dieu m'a a - se - - ne, Car touse ai trou -
30
il - li - ee De - üst o - re flou-rir
ve - e, Li - ant es - cha - laz: Un - ques
35
cueil - - lir Et un cha - pe - let ba - - stir
d'el n'i ot par - le, Mes souz moi l'ai ge -
40
A mes biaus che - veus te - - nir! S'en fus - se plus jo -
te - - e, Et quant j'oi le jeu fi - ne,

45
50
li - ne!' Lors l'a choi - si, s'est sail- - li - e:
Sa dist or: 'A- vez mout con - que - ste Qui m'a - vez
55
'Bien ve - gniez' fait il, 'm'a - - mi - e Que je
de - stour - be - - e?' Je li dis: 'En -
60
tant de - sir A te - nir Souz le rain; Mi -
si n'est pas; Be - le, si vos vient a gre
65
gno - te - ment la voi ve - nir Ce - le que j'aim.'
J'a - bi - te - rai le bois rame Tout a mes braz!'

Paris, Bibl. nat., Nouv. acq. fr. 13521 f. 369 recto (p. 729)

Paris, Bibl. nat., Nouv. acq. fr. 13521 f. 369 verso (p. 730)

Paris, Bibl. nat., Nouv. acq. fr. 13521 f. 370 recto (p. 731)

Paris, Bibl. nat., Nouv. acq. fr. 13521 f. 370 verso (p. 732)

Paris, Bibl. nat., Nouv. acq. fr. 13521 f. 371 recto (p. 733)

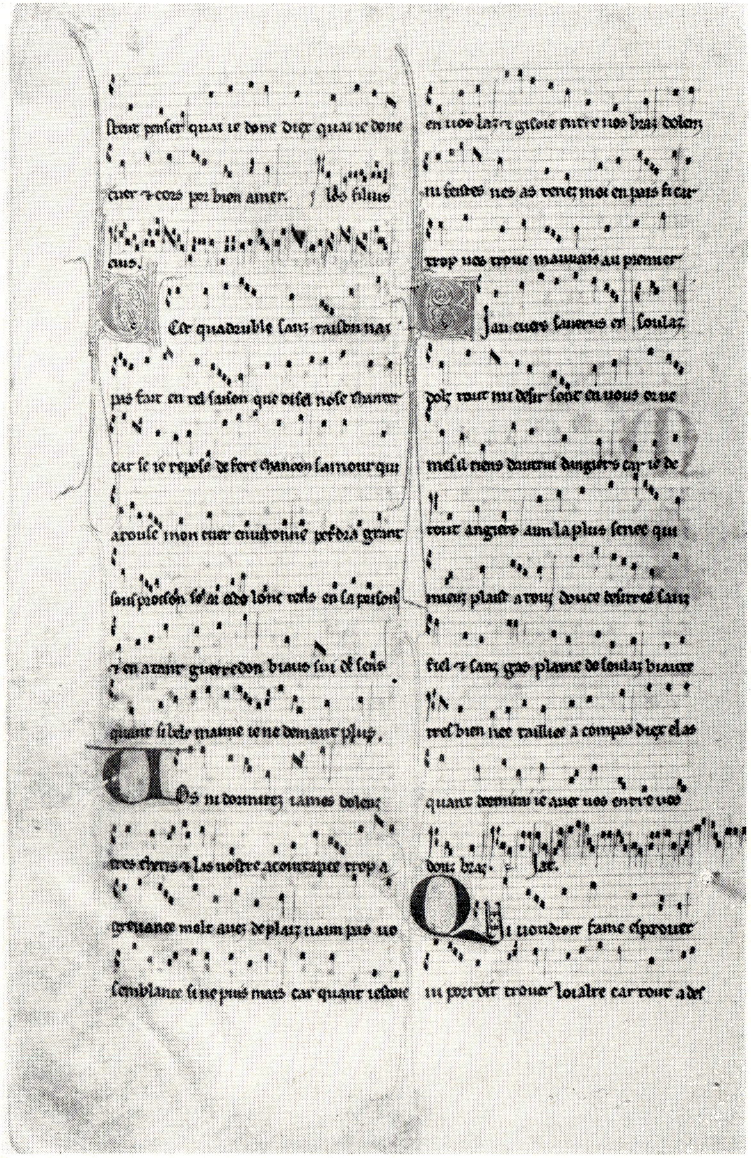

Paris, Bibl. nat., Nouv. acq. fr. 13521 f. 371 verso (p. 734)

Paris, Bibl. nat., Nouv. acq. fr. 13521 f. 372 recto (p. 735)

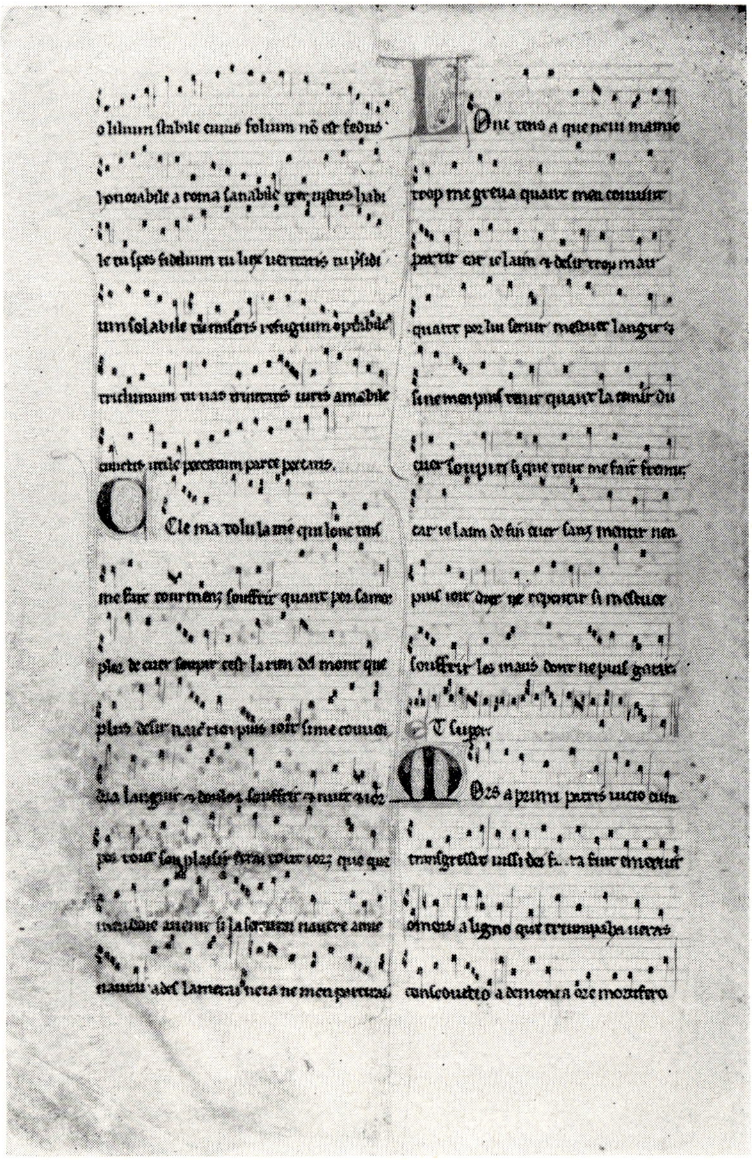

Paris, Bibl. nat., Nouv. acq. fr. 13521 f. 372 verso (p. 736)

Paris, Bibl. nat., Nouv. acq. fr. 13521 f. 373 recto (p. 737)

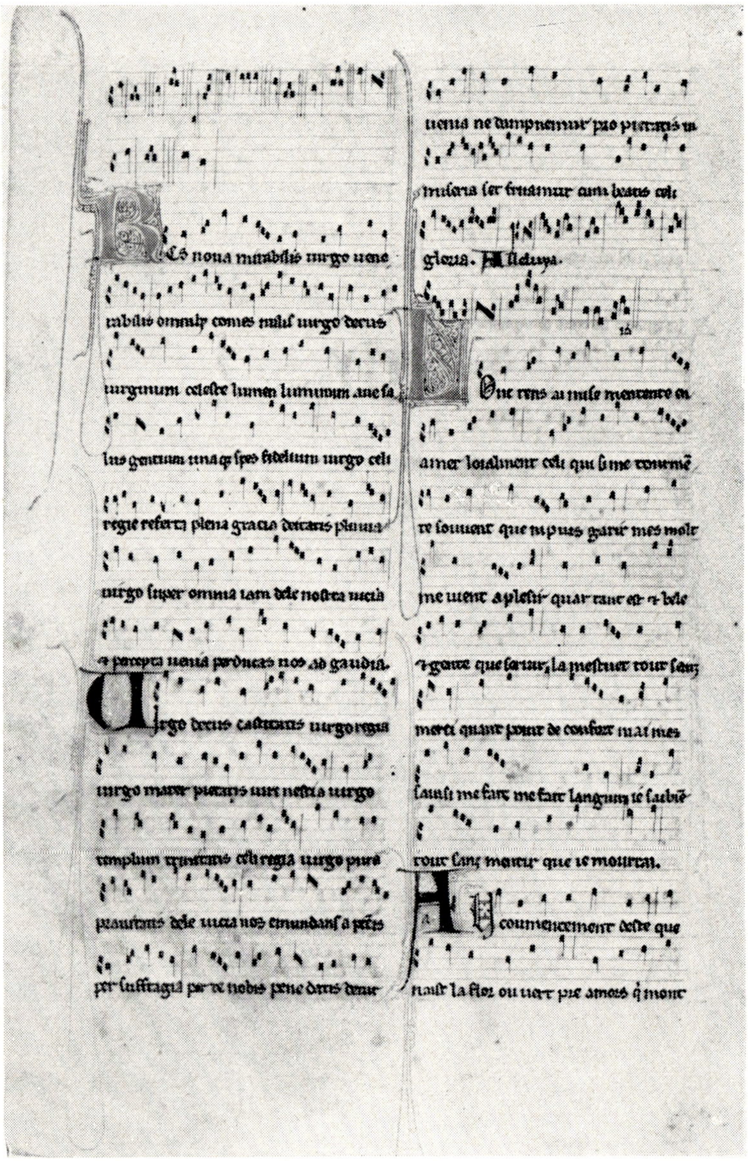

Paris, Bibl. nat., Nouv. acq. fr. 13521 f. 373 verso (p. 738)

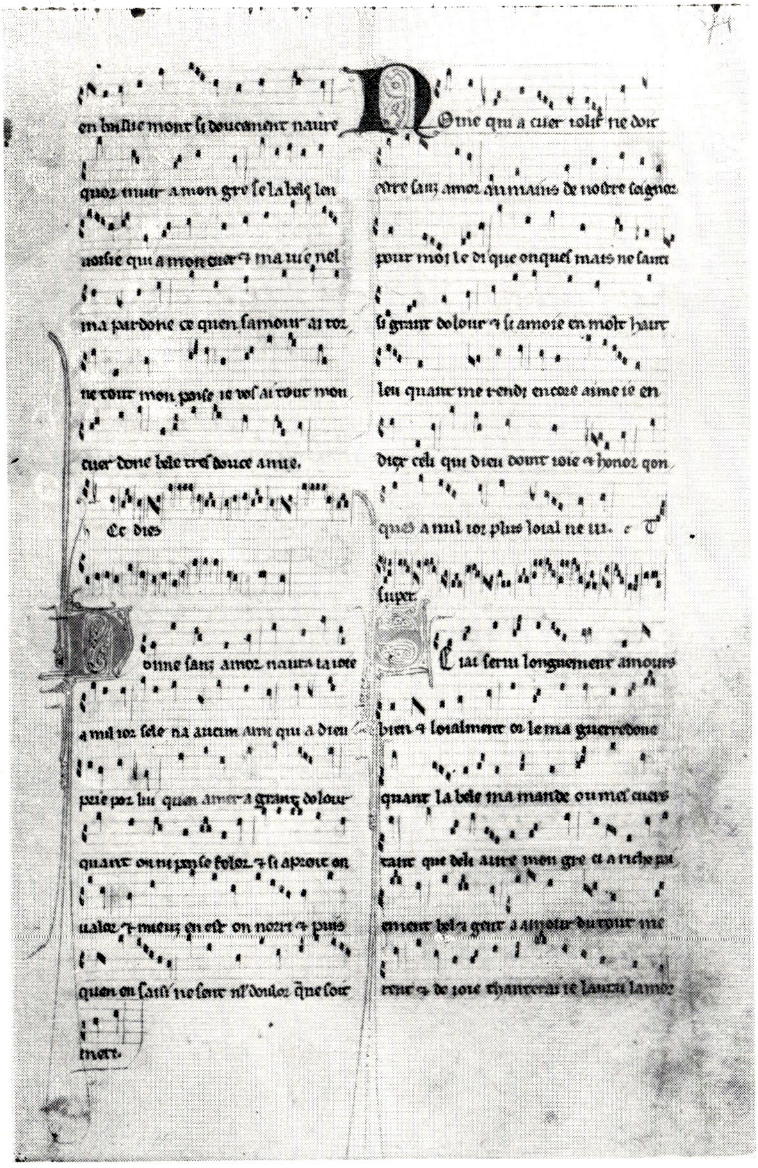

Paris, Bibl. nat., Nouv. acq. fr. 13521 f. 374 recto (p. 739)

Paris, Bibl. nat., Nouv. acq. fr. 13521 f. 374 verso (p. 740)

Paris, Bibl. nat., Nouv. acq. fr. 13521 f. 375 recto (p. 741)

Paris, Bibl. nat., Nouv. acq. fr. 13521 f. 375 verso (p. 742)

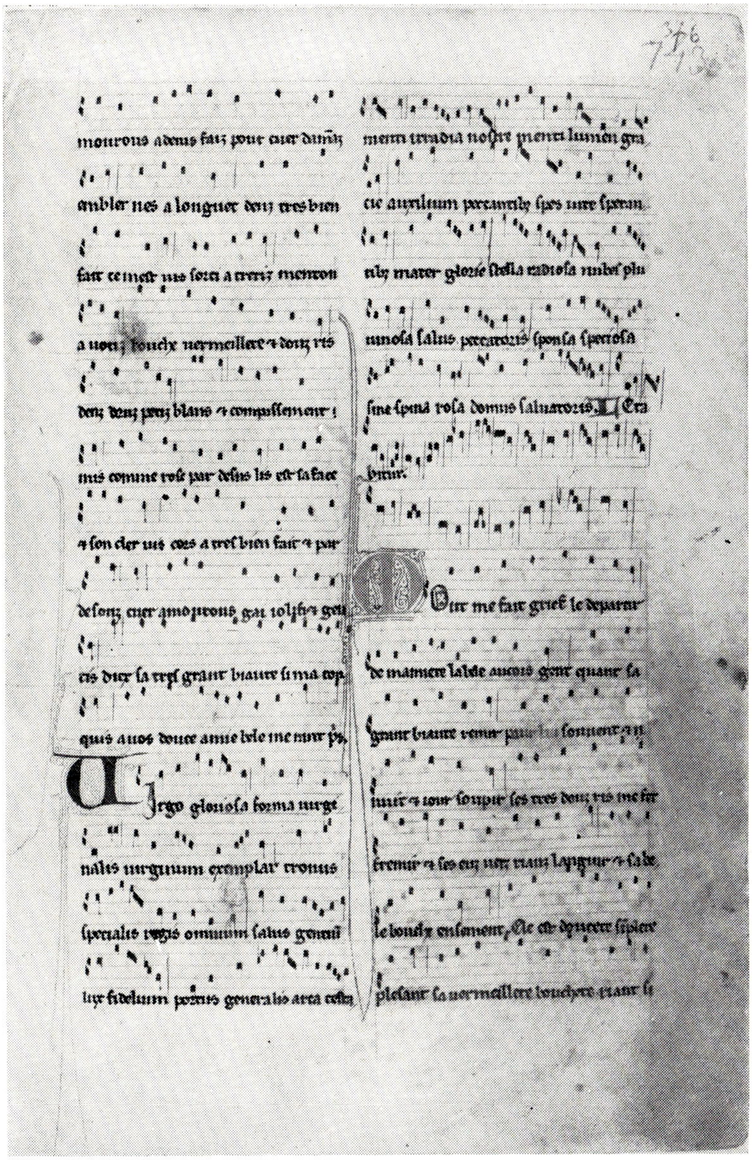

Paris, Bibl. nat., Nouv. acq. fr. 13521 f. 376 recto (p. 743)

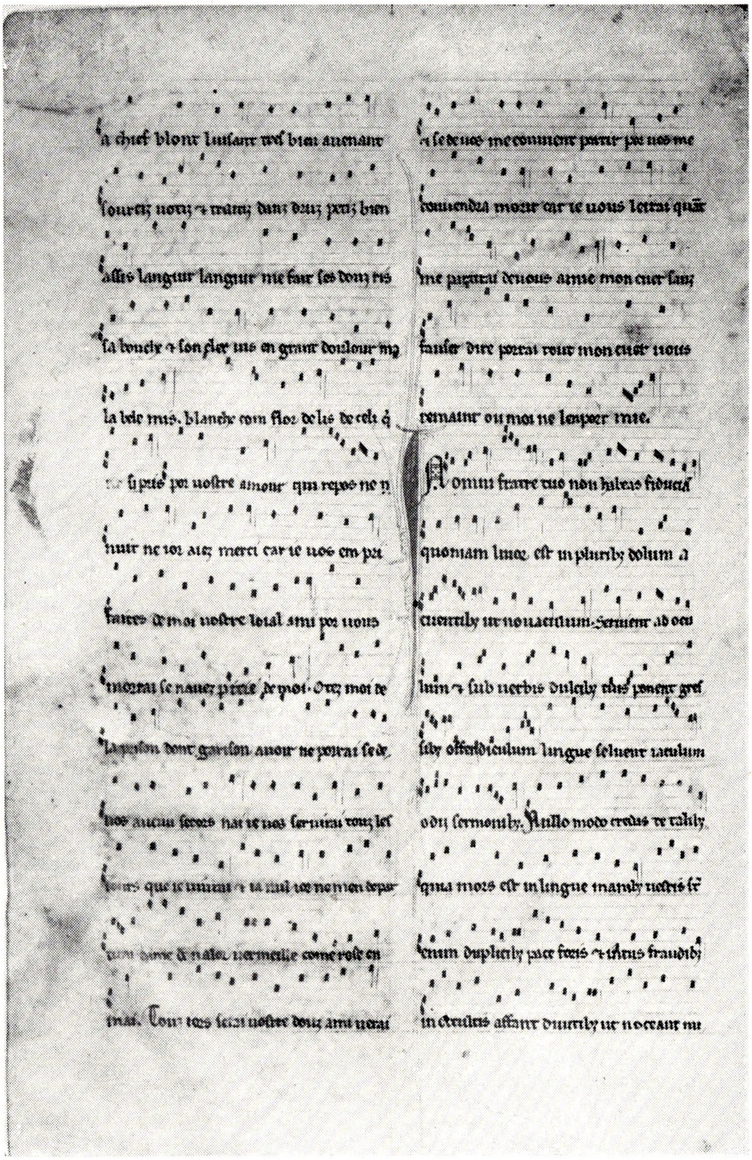

Paris, Bibl. nat., Nouv. acq. fr. 13521 f. 376 verso (p. 744)

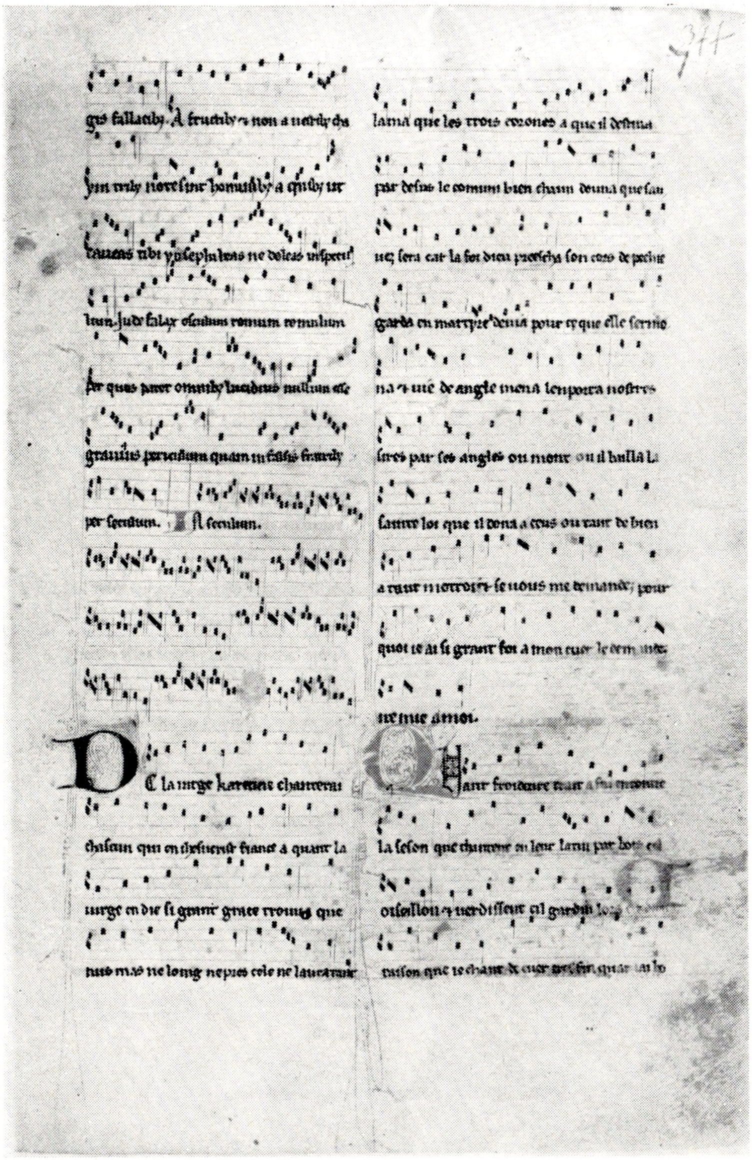

Paris, Bibl. nat., Nouv. acq. fr. 13521 f. 377 recto (p. 745)

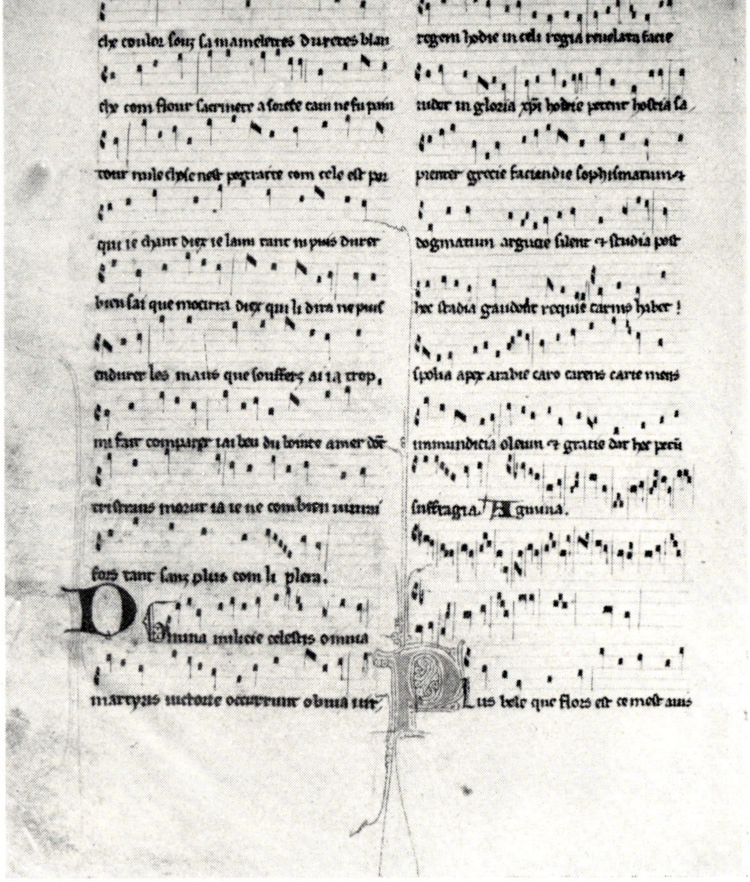

Paris, Bibl. nat., Nouv. acq. fr. 13521 f. 377 verso (p. 746)

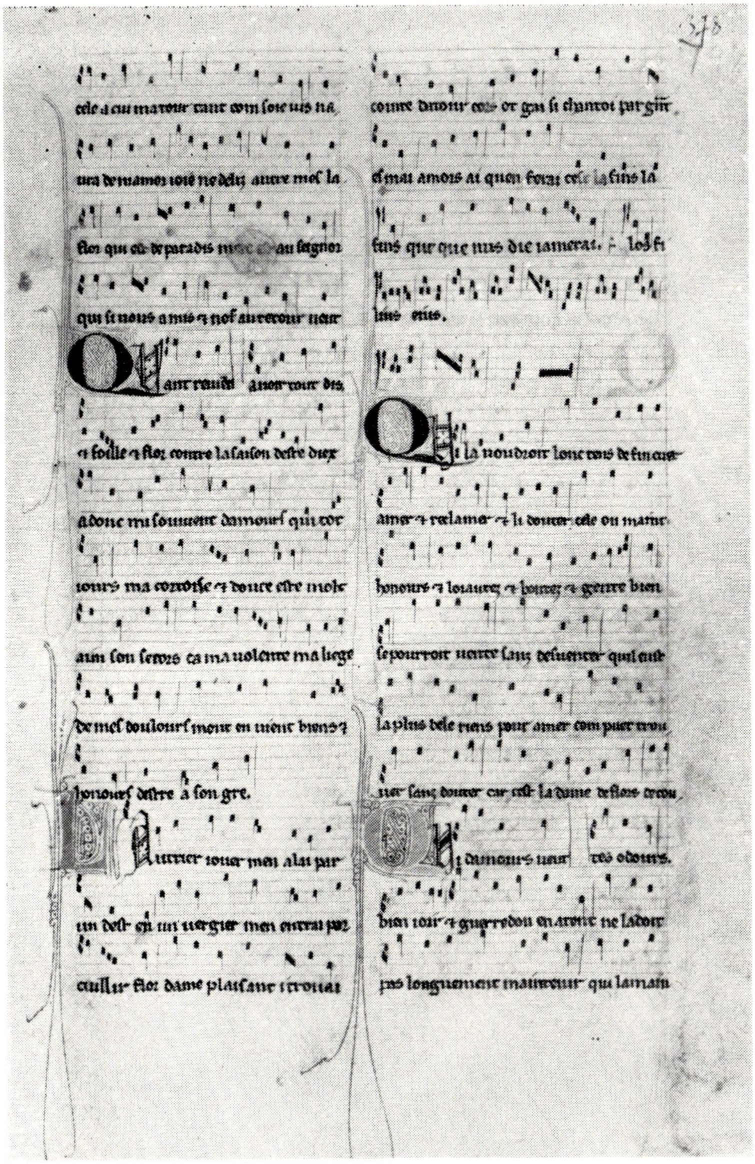

Paris, Bibl. nat., Nouv. acq. fr. 13521 f. 378 recto (p. 747)

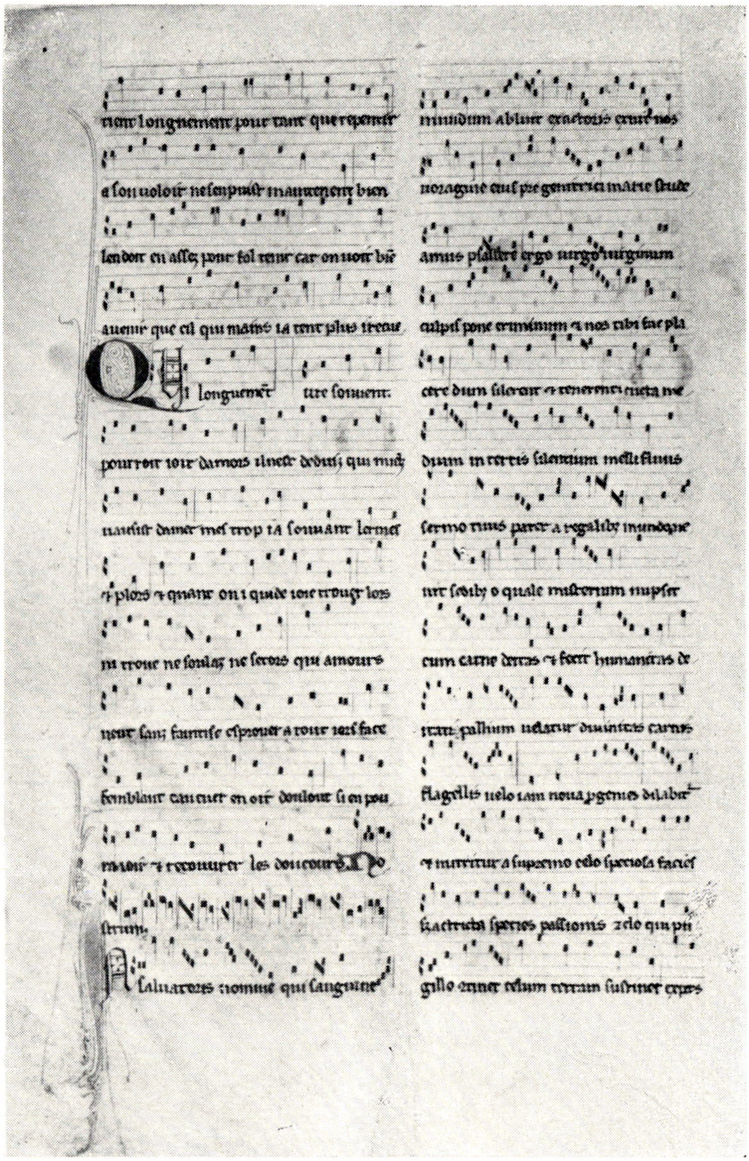

Paris, Bibl. nat., Nouv. acq. fr. 13521 f. 378 verso (p. 748)

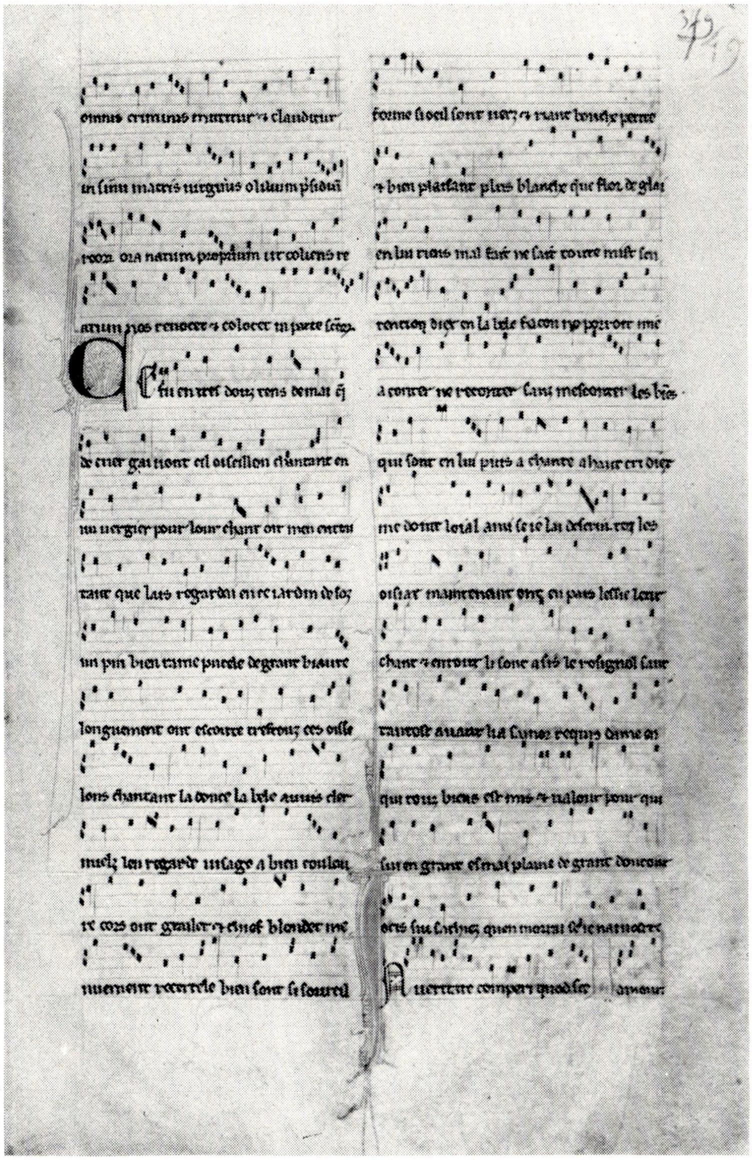

Paris, Bibl. nat., Nouv. acq. fr. 13521 f. 379 recto (p. 749)

Paris, Bibl. nat., Nouv. acq. fr. 13521 f. 379 verso (p. 750)

Paris, Bibl. nat., Nouv. acq. fr. 13521 f. 380 recto (p. 751)

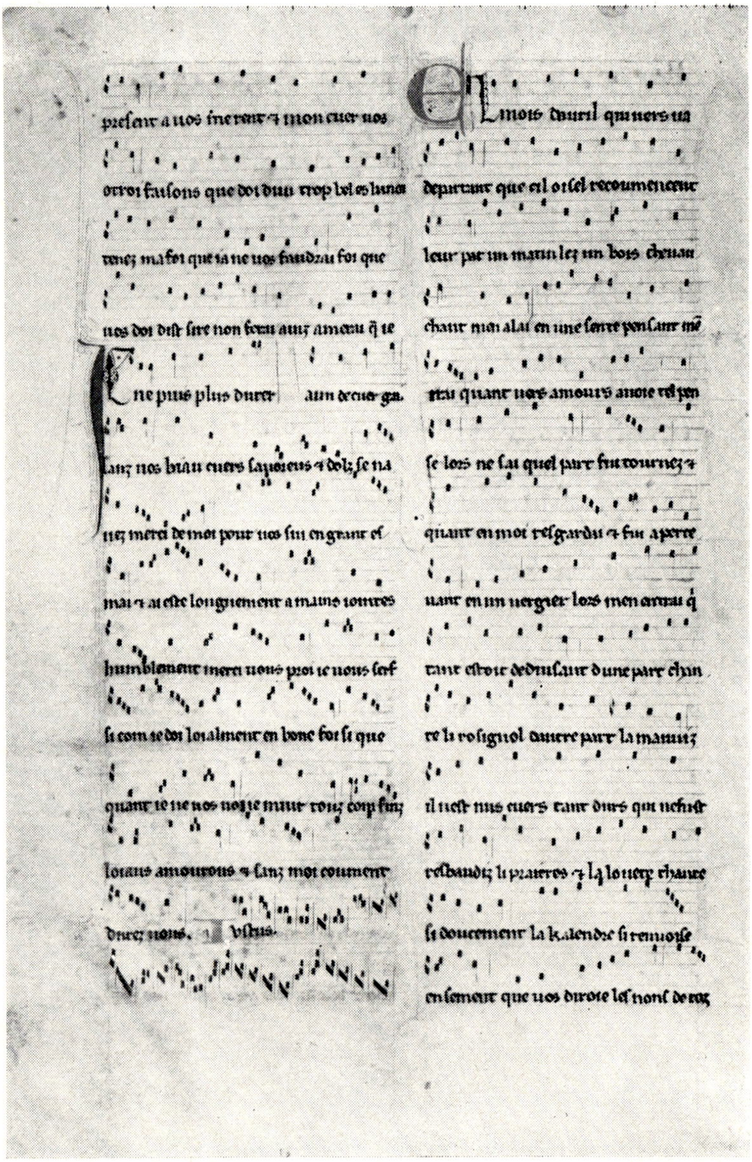

Paris, Bibl. nat., Nouv. acq. fr. 13521 f. 380 verso (p. 752)

Paris, Bibl. nat., Nouv. acq. fr. 13521 f. 381 recto (p. 753)

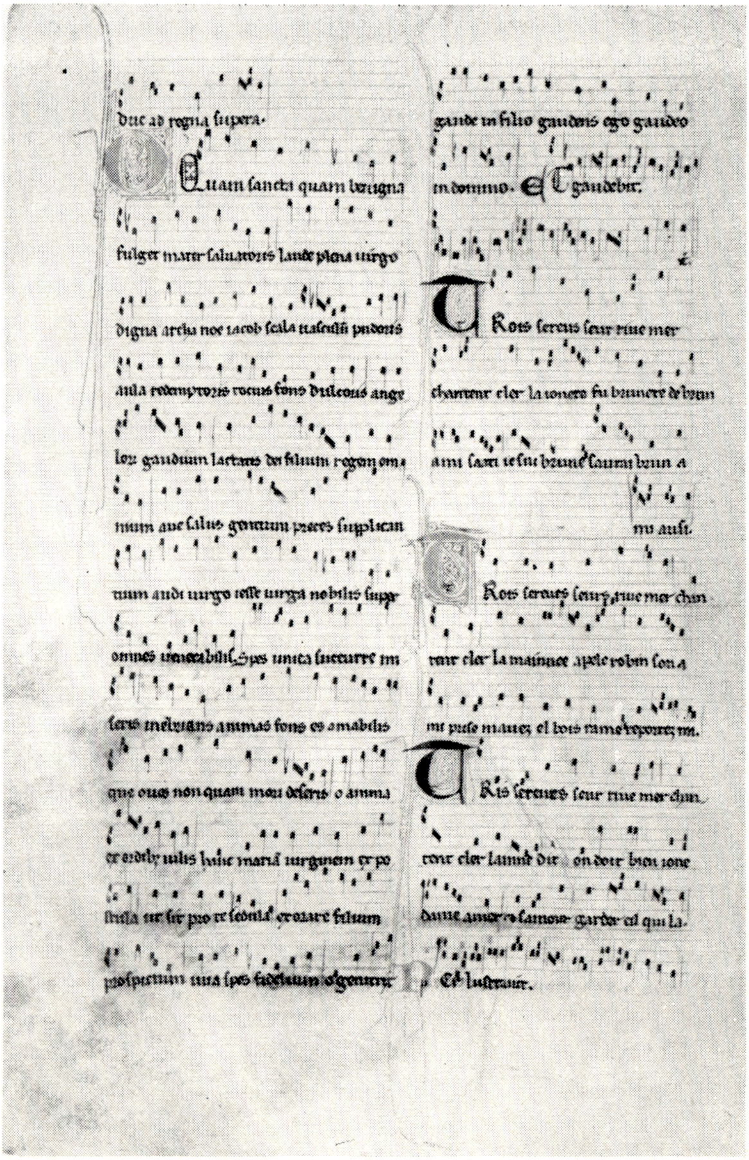

Paris, Bibl. nat., Nouv. acq. fr. 13521 f. 381 verso (p. 754)

Paris, Bibl. nat., Nouv. acq. fr. 13521 f. 382 recto (p. 755)

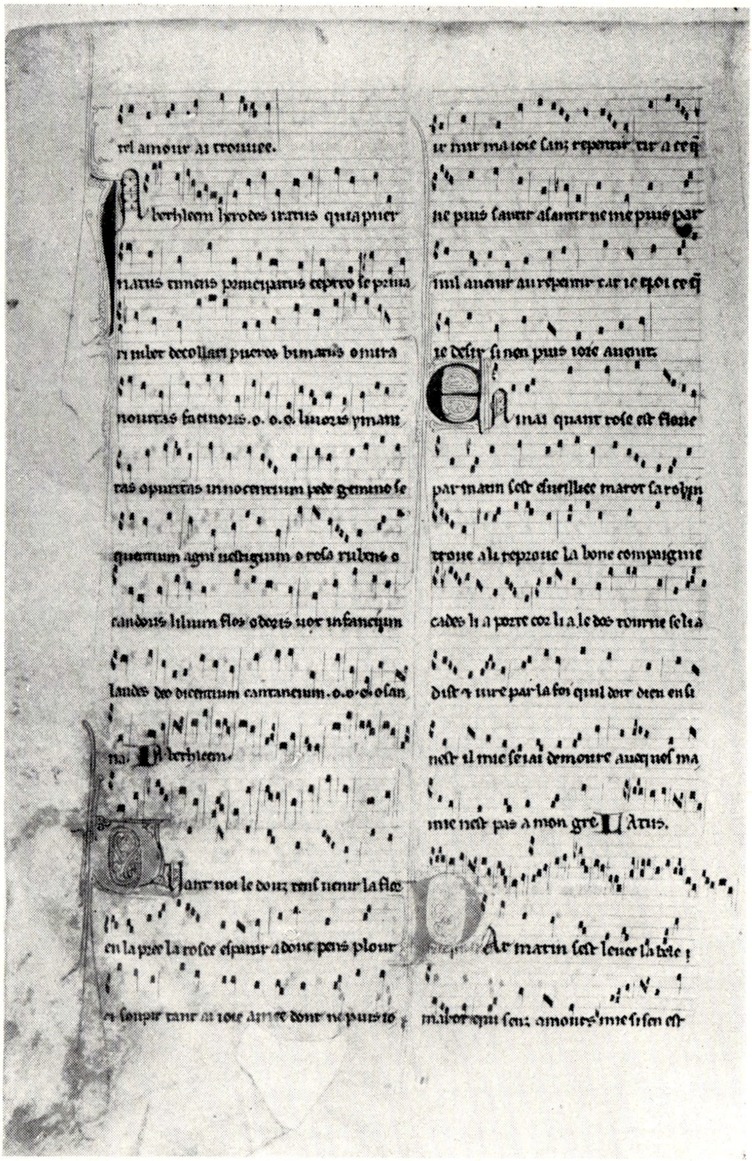

Paris, Bibl. nat., Nouv. acq. fr. 13521 f. 382 verso (p. 756)

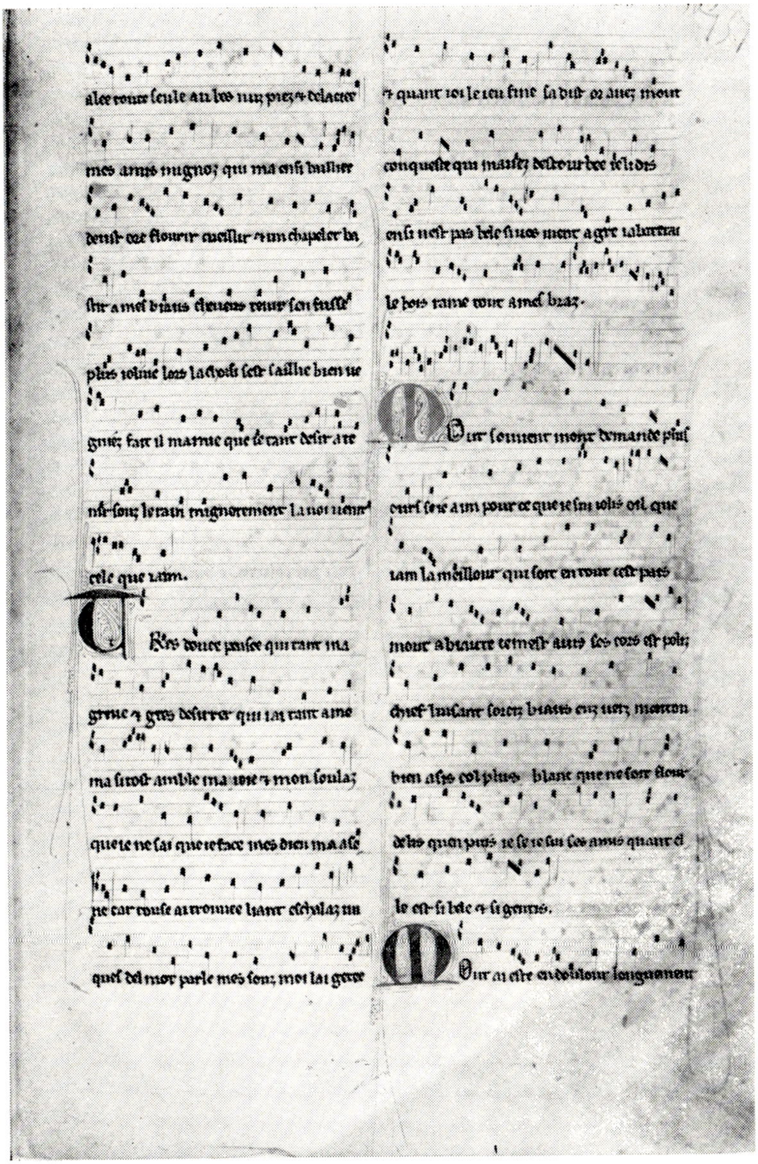

Paris, Bibl. nat., Nouv. acq. fr. 13521 f. 383 recto (p. 757)

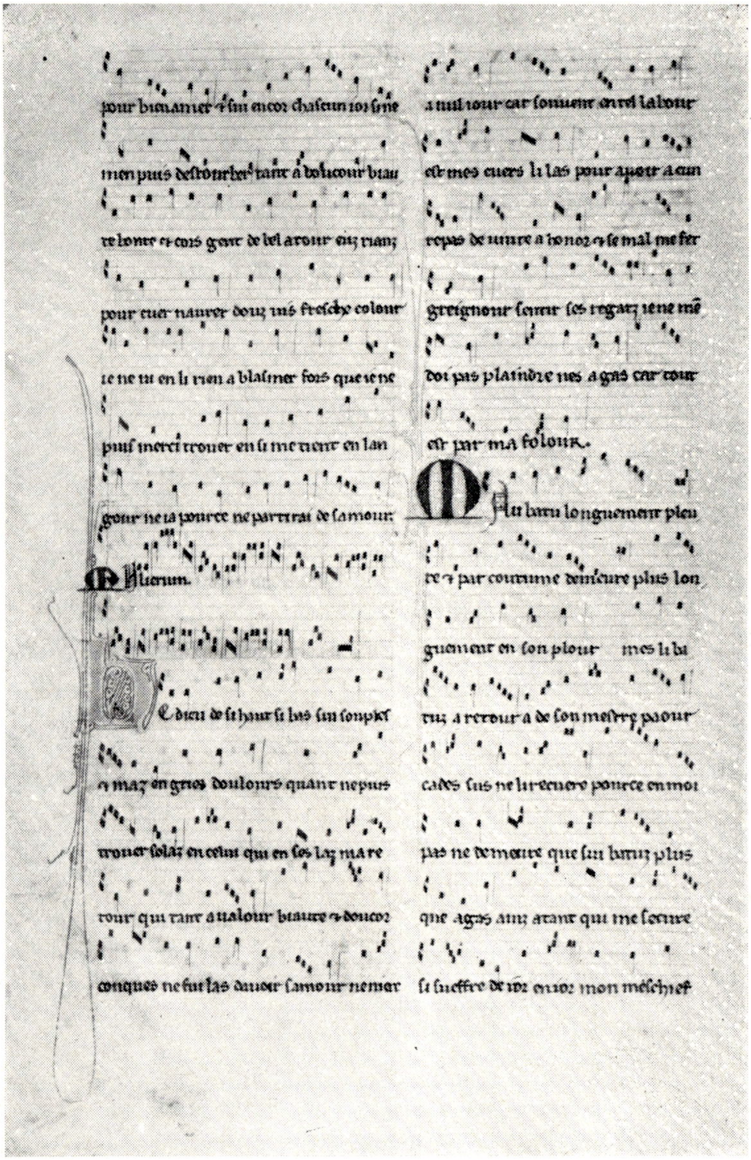

Paris, Bibl. nat., Nouv. acq. fr. 13521 f. 383 verso (p. 758)

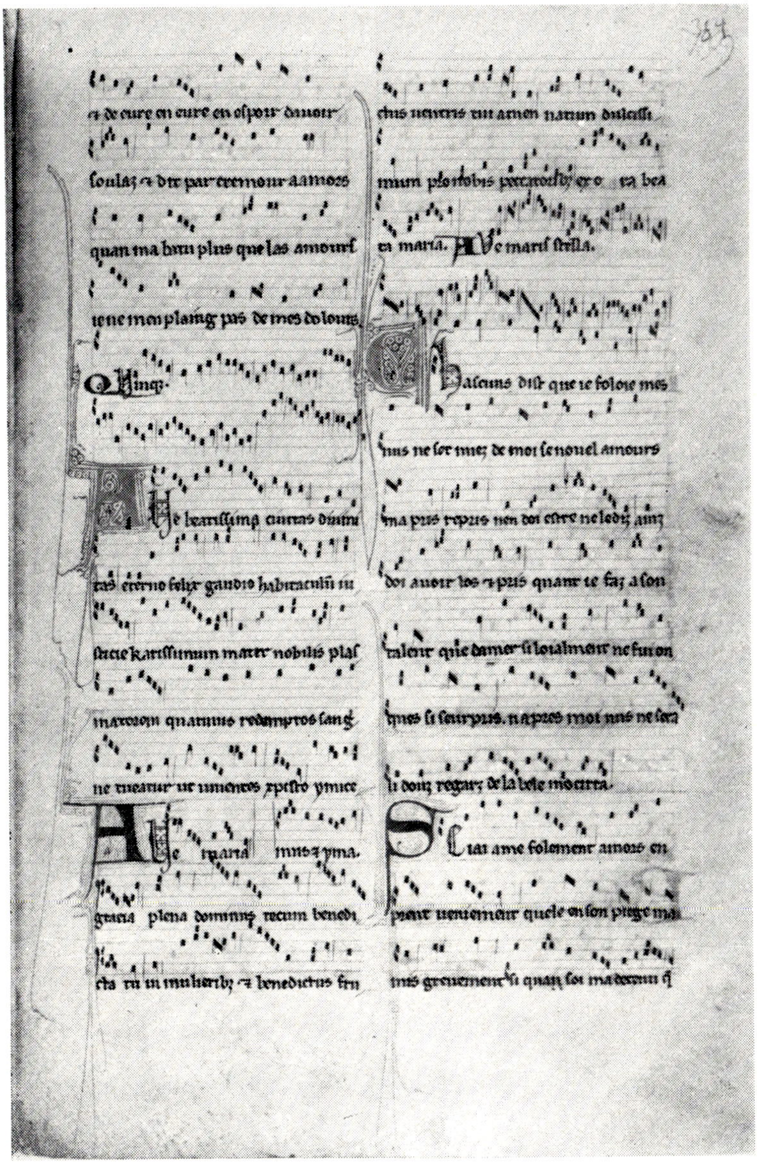

Paris, Bibl. nat., Nouv. acq. fr. 13521 f. 384 recto (p. 759)

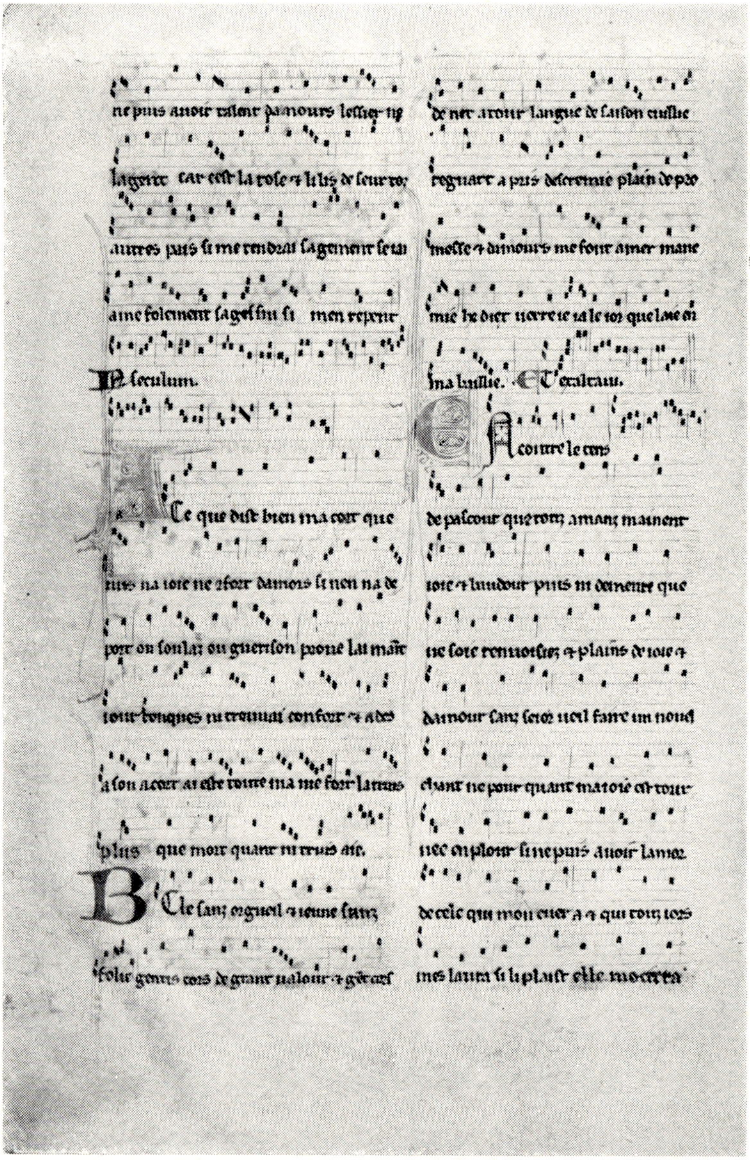

Paris, Bibl. nat., Nouv. acq. fr. 13521 f. 384 verso (p. 760)

Paris, Bibl. nat., Nouv. acq. fr. 13521 f. 385 recto (p. 761)

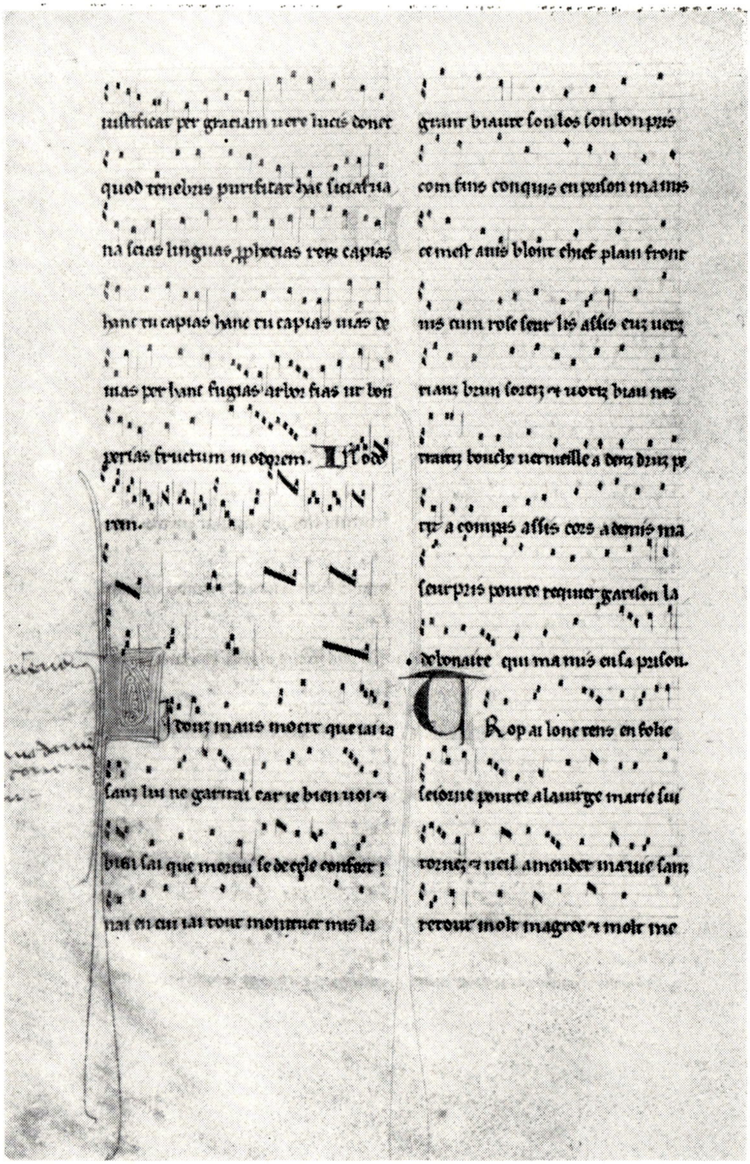

Paris, Bibl. nat., Nouv. acq. fr. 13521 f. 385 verso (p. 762)

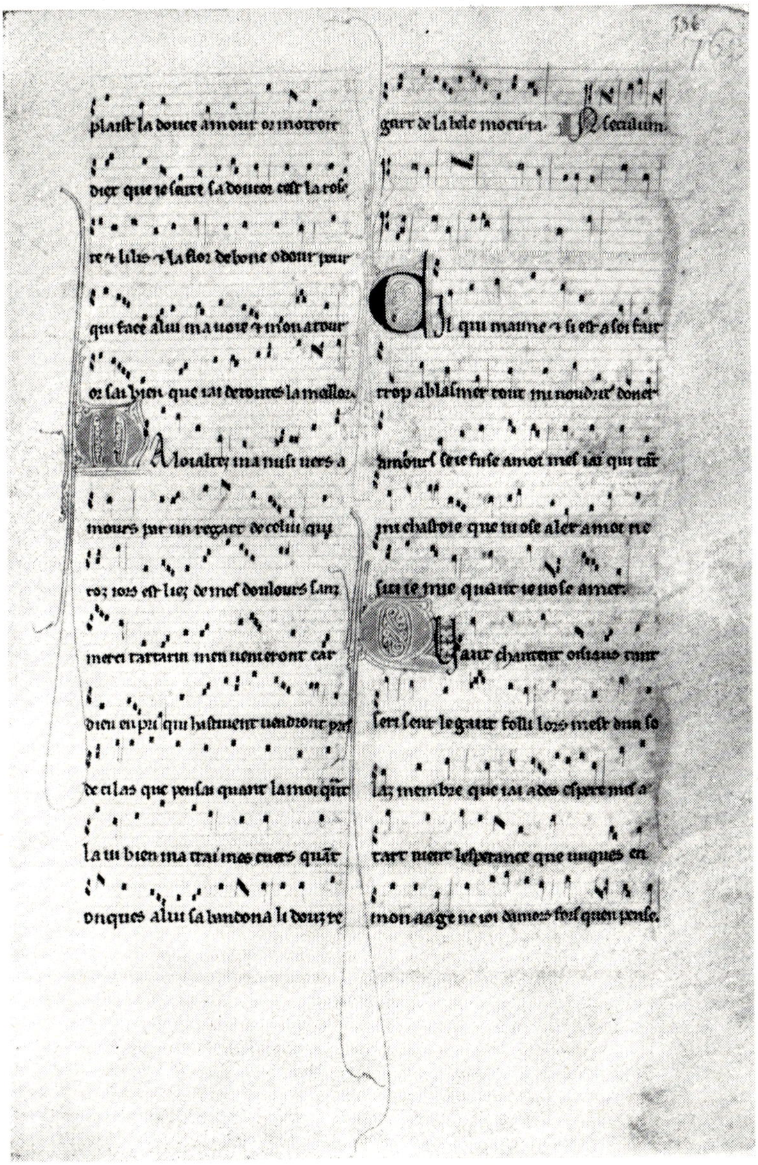

Paris, Bibl. nat., Nouv. acq. fr. 13521 f. 386 recto (p. 763)

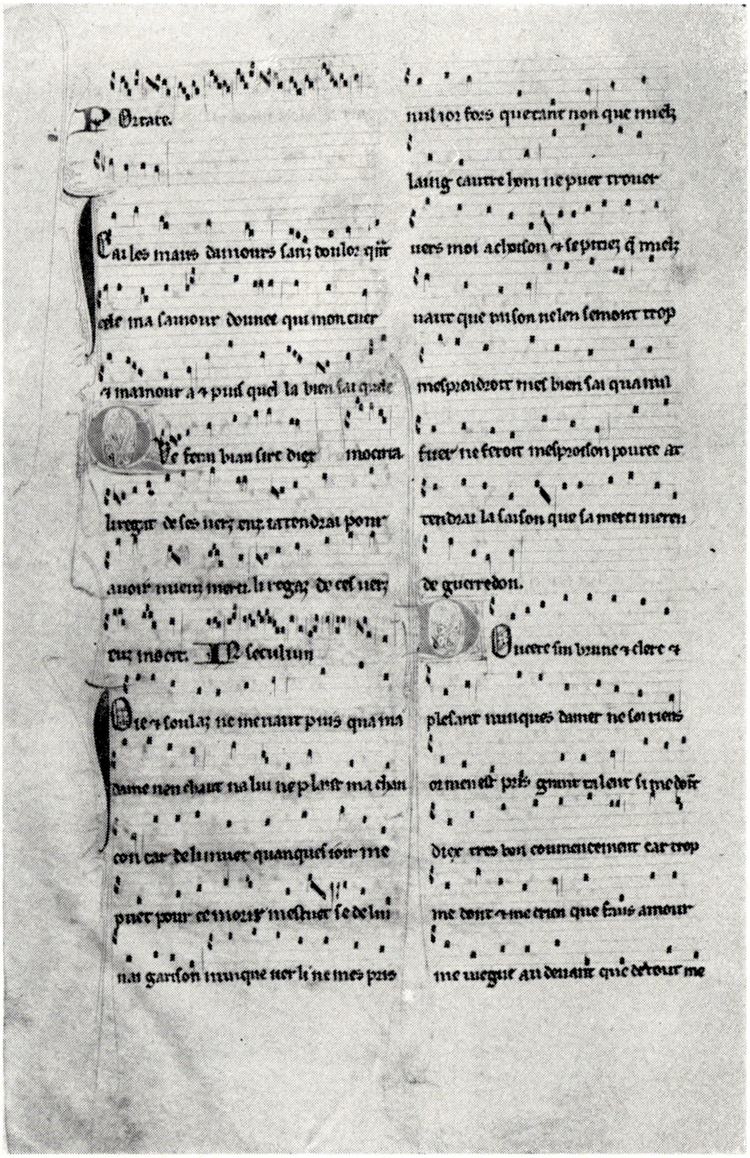

Paris, Bibl. nat., Nouv. acq. fr. 13521 f. 386 verso (p. 764)

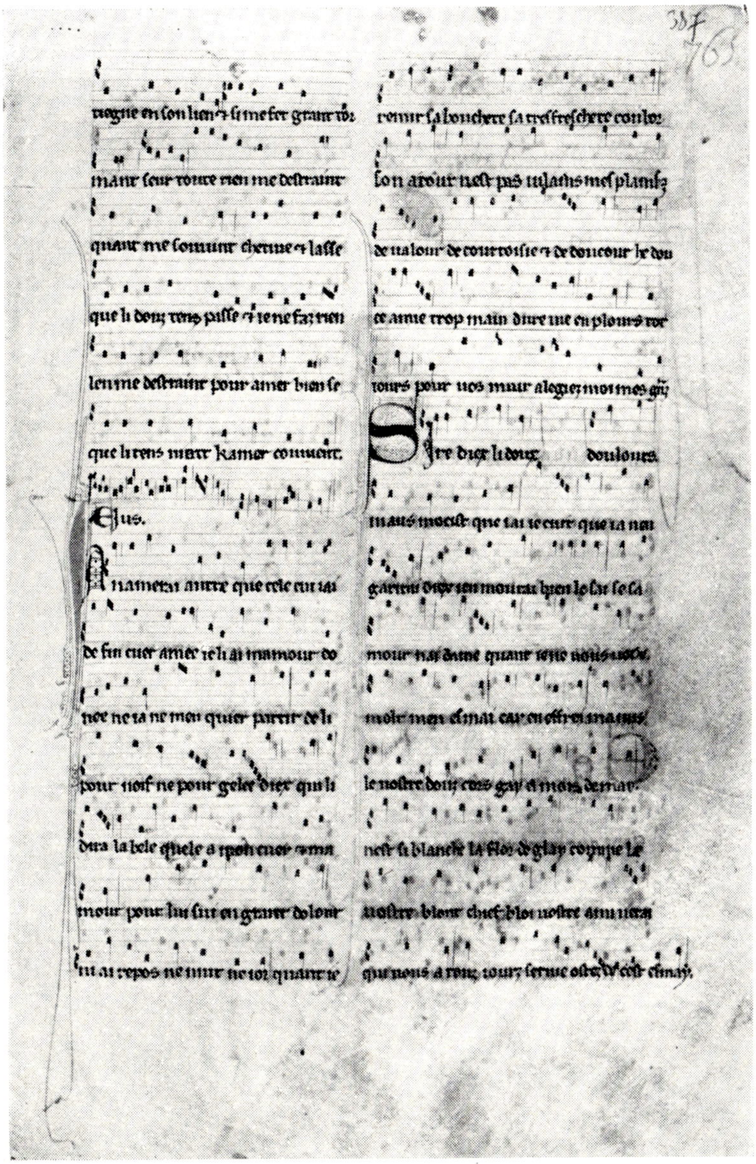

Paris, Bibl. nat., Nouv. acq. fr. 13521 f. 387 recto (p. 765)

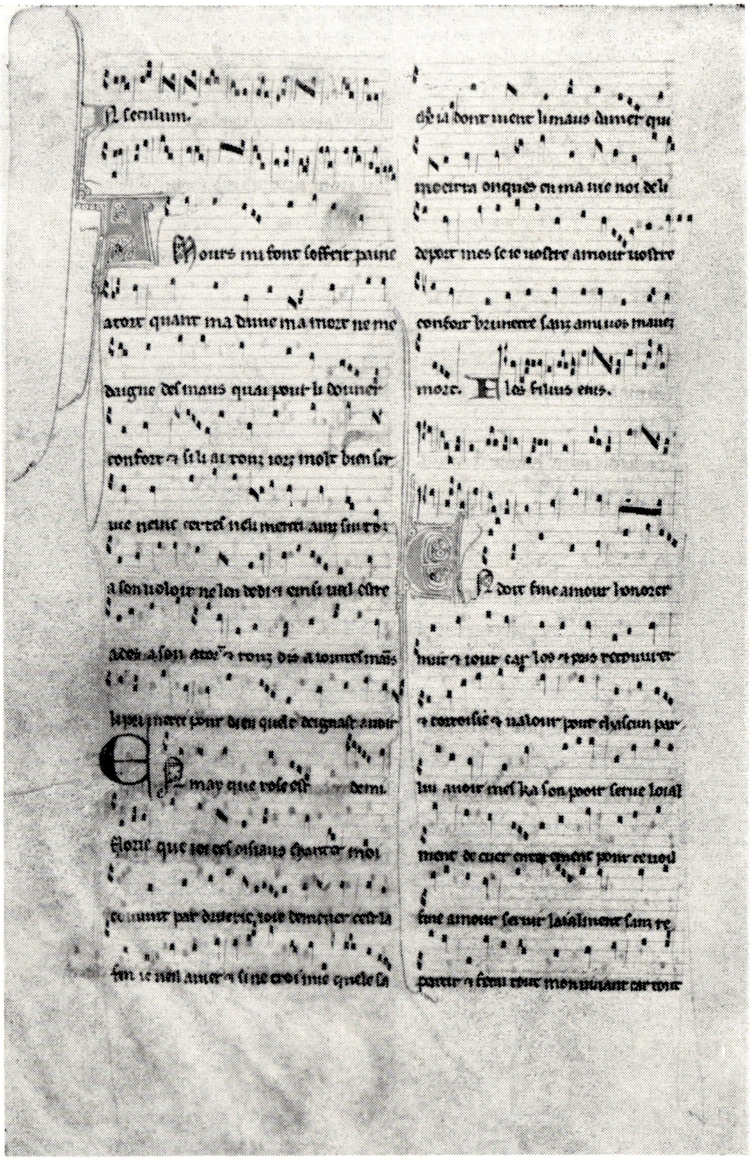

Paris, Bibl. nat., Nouv. acq. fr. 13521 f. 387 verso (p. 766)

Paris, Bibl. nat., Nouv. acq. fr. 13521 f. 388 recto (p. 767)

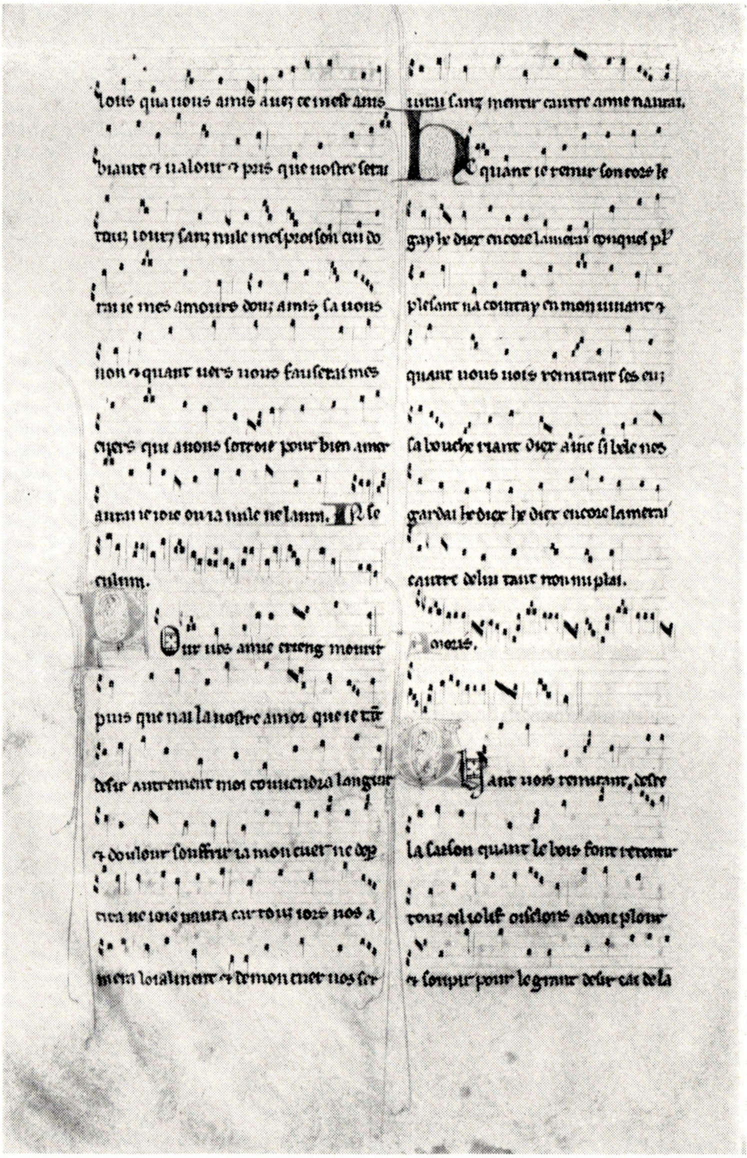

Paris, Bibl. nat., Nouv. acq. fr. 13521 f. 388 verso (p. 768)

Paris, Bibl. nat., Nouv. acq. fr. 13521 f. 389 recto (p .769)

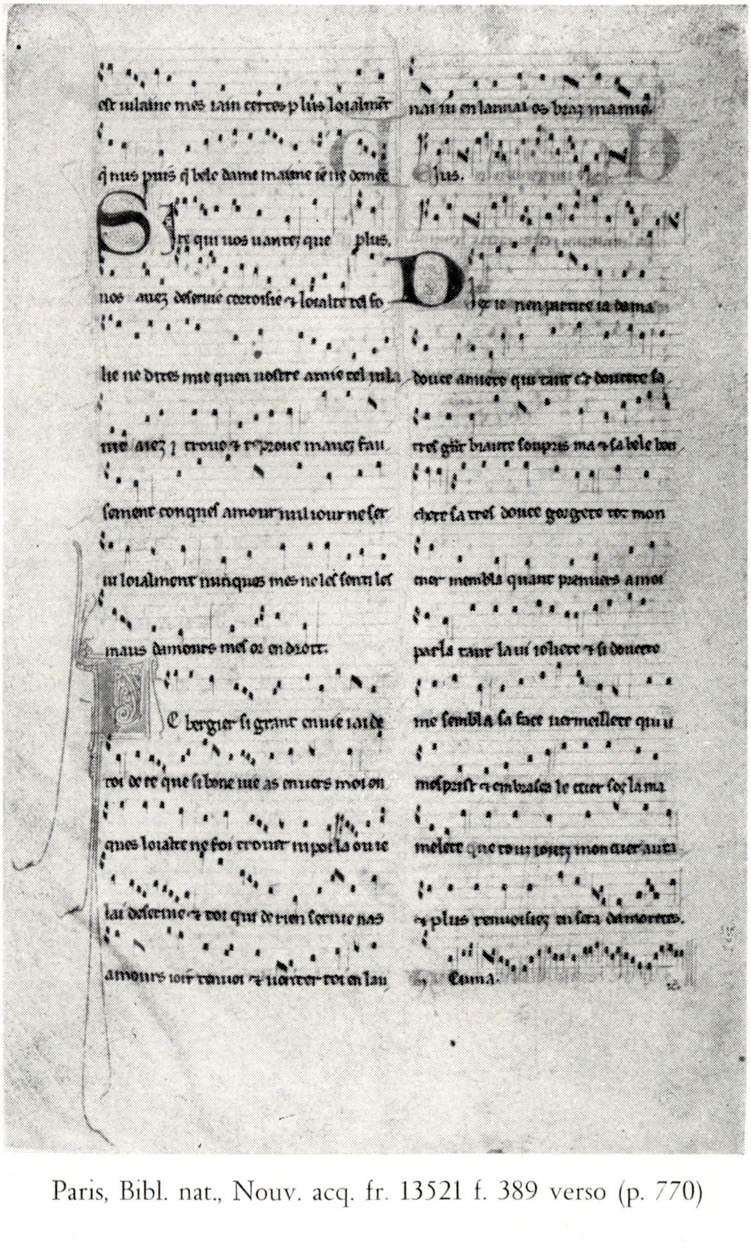

Paris, Bibl. nat., Nouv. acq. fr. 13521 f. 389 verso (p. 770)

Paris, Bibl. nat., Nouv. acq. fr. 13521 f. 390 recto (p. 771)

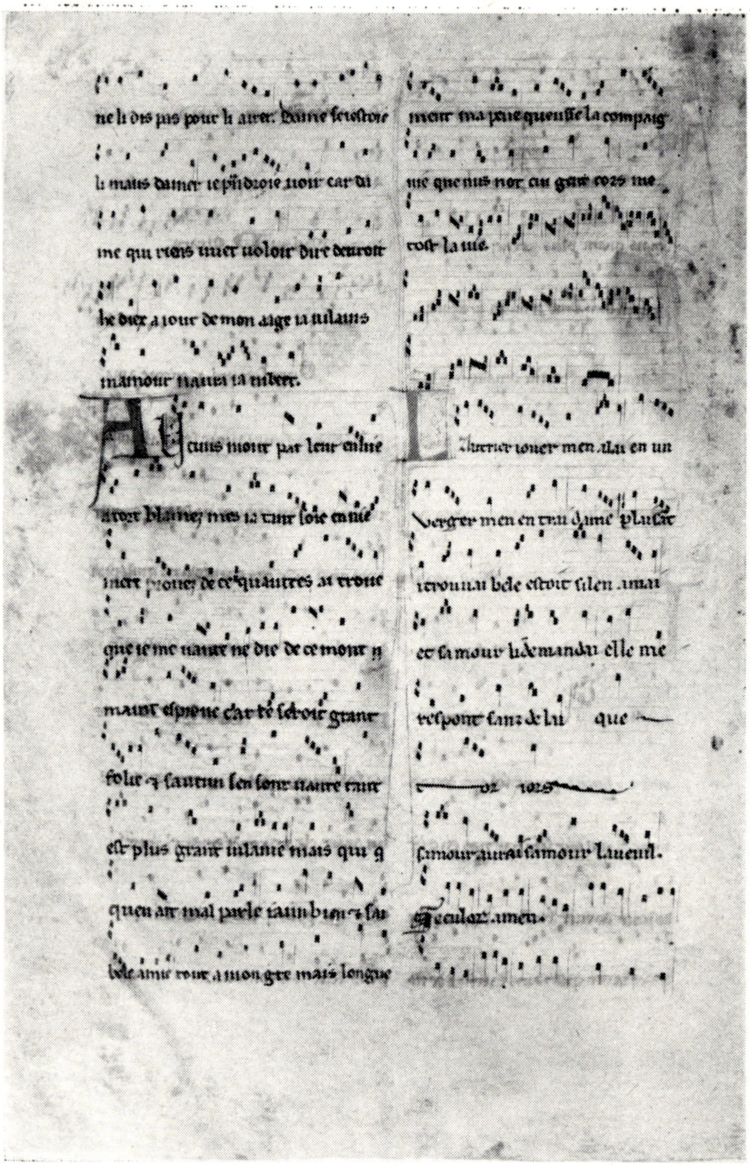

Paris, Bibl. nat., Nouv. acq. fr. 13521 f. 390 verso (p. 772)

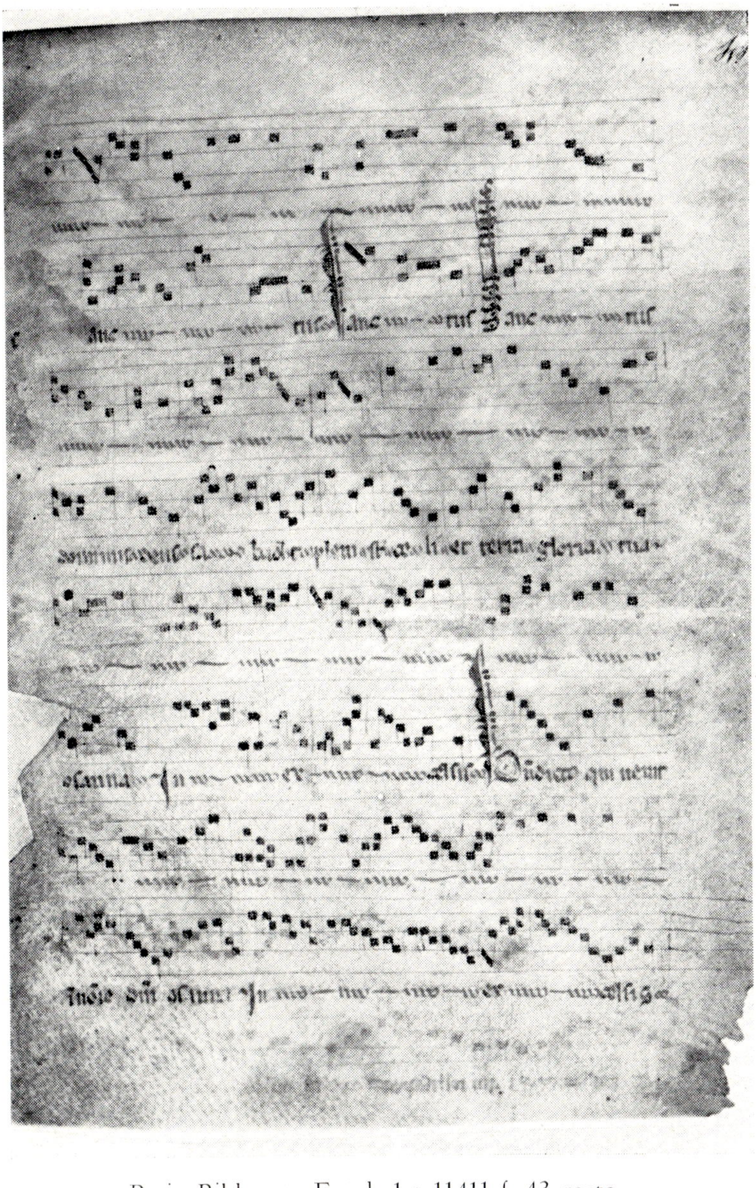

Paris, Bibl. nat., Fonds lat 11411 f. 43 recto

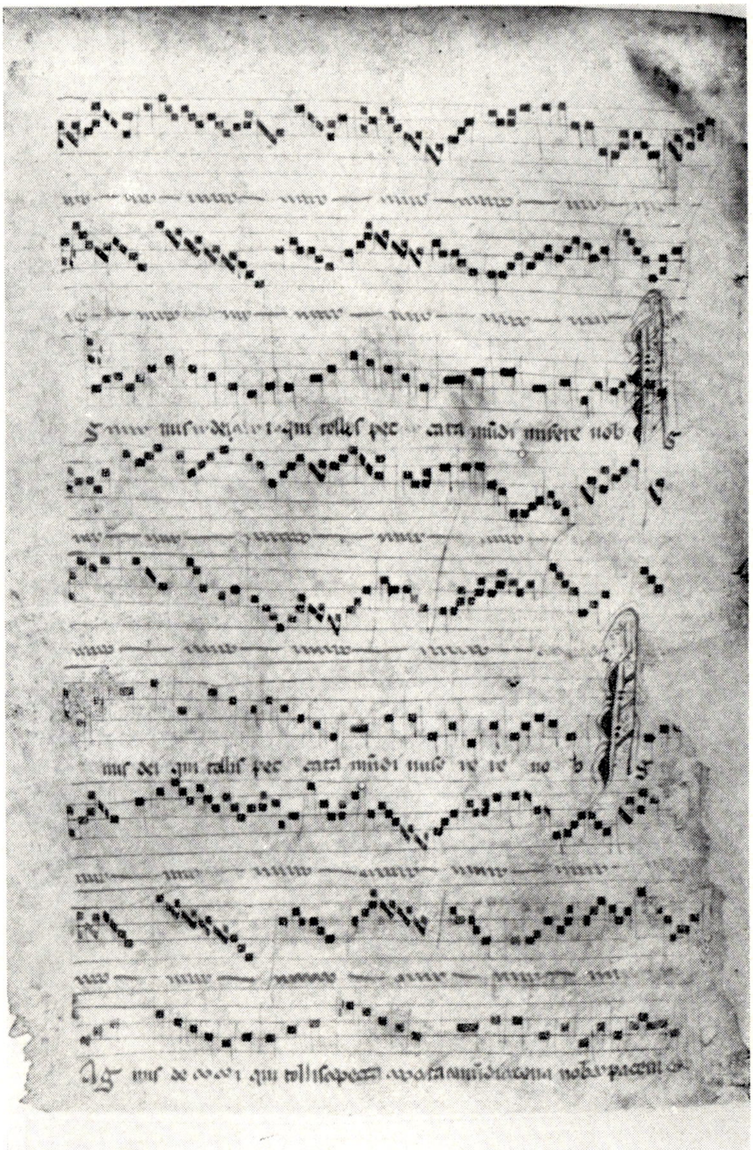

Paris, Bibl. nat., Fonds lat 11411 f. 43 verso

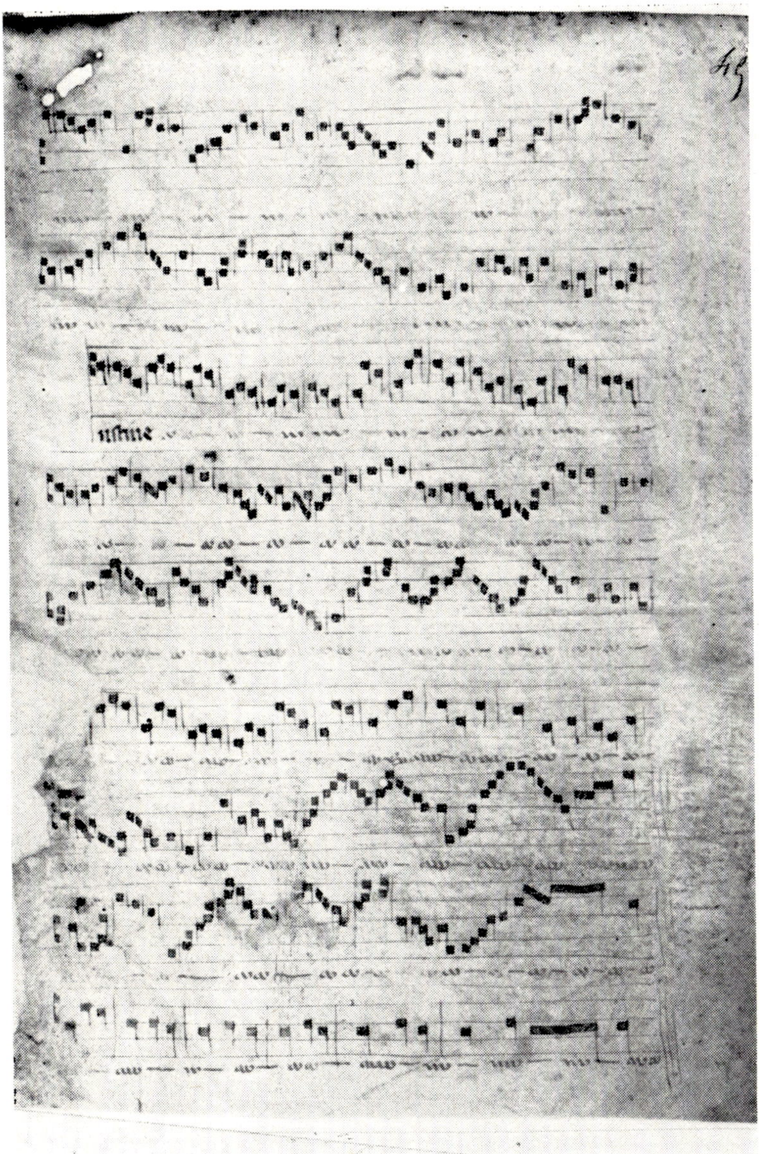

Paris, Bibl. nat., Fonds lat 11411 f. 44 recto

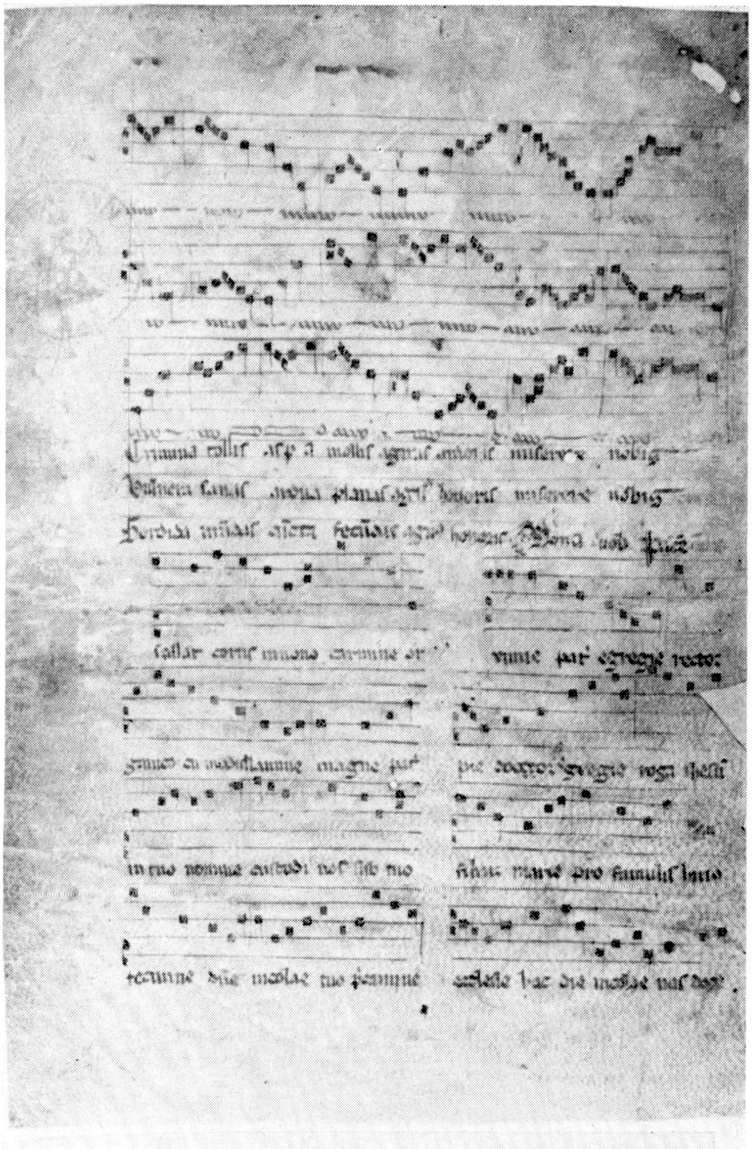

Paris, Bibl. nat., Fonds lat 11411 f. 44 verso

n. a. frç. 13521 Nr. 50

Mout m'a fait cruieus He Diex tant sui Gentes

25
Si m'a ra - me - ne De bas en haut, de plor en
li - ez So - loie e - stre et en - voi-siez Et jo-lif
30
chant; Sa dou - ce bou - che ri - ant, Vou-tis so -
nuit et jour. Hor sui tot des- con -seil -liez Par
35
retz Et verz euz, cors a-ve - nant, Sor tou- te s'a - mour
ma fo - lour. Diex! car m'en - se - i - gniez
40
qui tant vaut M'a ga - ri: Si me tient le cuer baut.
Que puis - se re - cou - vrer per - due ai a - mour!

lat. 11411 Nr. 1 Sanctus

35
na in ex-
40
cel-
45
sis. Be - ne- di- ctus qui ve - nit in no - mi -
50
ne do - mi - ni. O - san - na In
55
ex-

lat. 11411 Nr. 2 Agnus Dei

10
qui tol- lis pec-
15
ca- ta mun- di
20
mi- se- re-
do- na no-
25
no- bis.
pa- cem
Fine

30
A- gnus de- i,
35
qui tol - lis pec- ca-
40
ta mun- di mi- se-
45
re re no- bis.
D.C.

lat. 11411 Nr. 3 Sustine

25
30
35
40

45
50
55
60

lat. 11411 Nr. 4 Crimina tollis

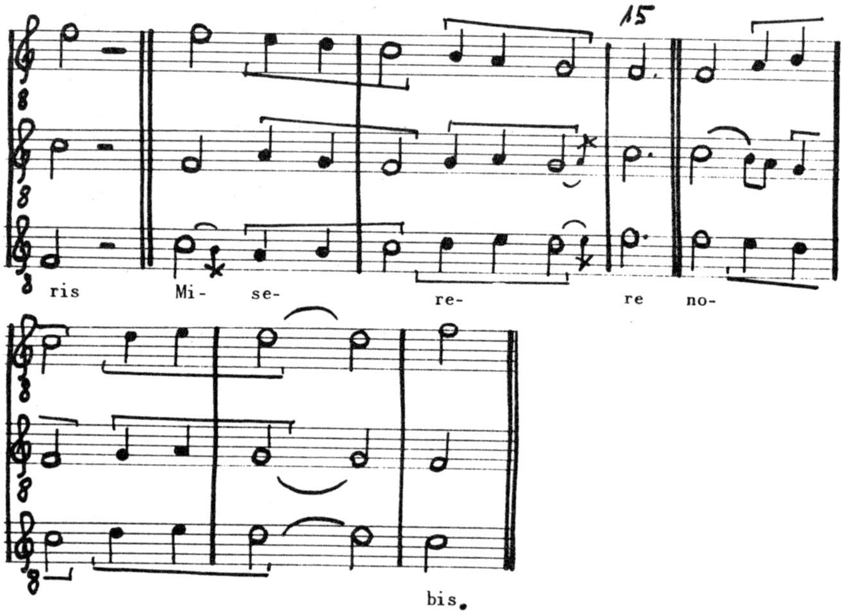

II. Vulnera sanas,
Ardua planas,
Agnus honoris.
Miserere nobis.

III. Sordida mundas,
Munda fecundas,
Agnus honoris.
Dona nobis pacem.

UNSERE VEROEFFENTLICHUNGEN
OUR PUBLICATIONS

VEROEFFENTLICHUNGEN MITTELALTERLICHER MUSIKHANDSCHRIFTEN

PUBLICATIONS OF MEDIAEVAL MUSICAL MANUSCRIPTS

Vol. I	Madrid 20486	$8.00
Vol. II	Wolfenbuettel 1099	
Vol. III	Eine zentrale Quelle der Notre-Dame Musik A Central Source of Notre-Dame Polyphony	$15
Vol. IV	Paris, nouv. acq. fr. 13521 & lat. 11411	$7.50
Vol. V	Worcester Add. 68, Westminster Abbey 33327 & Madrid 192	$9.00

Text: *Deutsch & English*

MUSICAL THEORISTS IN TRANSLATION

Vol. I	Anonymous IV	$7.50
Vol. II	Robert de Handlo	$7.00

Text: *English*

MIKROFILME MICROFILMS

I	Studies of Music in the Middle Ages (Gennrich, Wagner, Schwan, Appel, Sartori, Schneider & Raynaud)	$18
II	U. Chevalier, Repertorium Hymnologicum	$12

WISSENSCHAFTLICHE ABHANDLUNGEN
MEDIAEVAL STUDIES

I	L. Dittmer, Auszug aus 'The Worcester Music Fragments'	$1.00